MondayMorning
Prayers

David Faust

Design: Mike Helm

Faust, David M. 1954-

Monday Morning Prayers.

1. Prayers. 2. Christian Churches and Churches of Christ—Prayer-books and devotions. 3. Restoration Movement (Christianity)—Prayer-books and devotions. 4. Holidays—Prayer-books and devotions.

ISBN 978-0-615-40689-3

Publication made possible by a grant from the Arington Foundation. The entire purchase price of this book contributes to the Arington Scholarship Fund at Cincinnati Christian University, **www.CCUniversity.edu**.

To my granddaughters,
Abbie and Kayla.
May you always walk with God.

Contents

Prayers to Start the Work-Week

Prayers for Special Days and Seasons

Foreword

If you sit down and speak with someone who is older than you are, you will hear something about how times were simpler "back then." "Back then" could mean 1977. It could mean 1964. It could mean 1942. It could even mean 1998.

No matter when you were born, life clips on at a quicker pace than it used to. Progress has pushed efficiency into its highest levels on record, which means that nearly everything done today moves faster and more streamlined than it used to move.

Consider the simple example of a family dinner. Two hundred years ago, preparation for cooking the evening meal began in the morning, maybe even before the sun came up. Fifty years ago, with the dawn of modern appliances, a caring mother could delay dinner preparations until later in the afternoon. And today, you can go from hungry to eating a warm meal in 90 seconds, thanks to your trusty microwave.

Things are more efficient today. But that doesn't necessarily mean things are better—for your soul, at least. One of the unintended consequences of modern

Relationships cannot be built quickly or without effort.

progress is that we now expect everything to move quickly. We grow impatient—even angry—when the red light takes too long to change. We sigh and glare at the person behind the counter when our "fast food" isn't fast enough for our jammed schedules. We watch a show on TV, and if it's boring for even a few seconds we quickly flip to another (equally boring) show. And then another. And then another. We click around on websites, taking in information at a remarkable pace. If we ever find ourselves stuck in a doctor's office waiting for an appointment, we quickly pull out our smart phones and catch up on our e-mail, text a few friends, and check the latest headlines.

Quicker. More efficient. Better.

But then we come to the little compartment in our lives marked "Soul." Despite our best efforts to avoid it, we can't deny that we are more than just electrons and neurons firing through a frontal lobe. We have feelings. We have desires. We have spiritual questions that reach beyond the physical limits of this world. We hit the boundaries of what this temporal life can offer us, and we search for something more. In the deepest parts of ourselves, we know that we are mere creations. And every creation must have a Creator. So we look for him.

Too often we approach our soul work, our spiritual search, with these same principles in mind. Quicker. More efficient. Better. It doesn't take long for frustration to set in because we come face to face with this painstaking truth: our Creator doesn't work like that. Where we push for quick growth, he slows us down and makes us take our time. Where we push for greater efficiency, he leads us on seemingly crooked paths. Where we strive to be better, he shows us our failures with greater clarity.

Why does God work like this?

Because he is not a project manager, driven by the bottom line. He is a loving Father, concerned about his relationship with us. And relationships cannot be built quickly or without effort.

So we pray. We open ourselves up to God and talk with him. We surrender our preferences for quickness and efficiency and project-like self-improvement for something better: a relationship with our great God. We pause. We take a break from our task lists. And we let the Creator of our souls continue his work—his slow, often confusing, often hidden work—in us.

The following pages are meant to help you with your attempt to slow down and be with God. May they be a blessing to your spiritual journey with him.

E. Thomas Arington
Chairman and CEO of Prasco Laboratories
Mason, Ohio

A NOTE TO THE READER

Monday mornings can be tough.

You see it in the eyes of business leaders as they head back to the office. You sense it in your kids as they brace themselves for another week of school. Blue collar and white collar workers alike carry the burdens of Monday morning as the weight of the work-week settles onto their shoulders.

In recent years the burdens seem even heavier. We didn't realize how good we had it back in the 1990s. Oh, we worried about Y2K and the possibility of a worldwide computer glitch when the clock ticked midnight on December 31, 1999. We complained about the economy, griped about our political leaders, and worried about Wall Street. But we didn't realize that thousands would lose their lives in the terrorist attacks of September 11, 2001. We didn't foresee that security measures would become more time-consuming or that we faced a recession and unprecedented economic turmoil.

But if we were paying attention, we realized a vital truth: *No matter what happens, we need God*. We need him in our marriages and families, in our careers and our relationships. We need him in our nation and in our neighborhood. We need him at work on Monday just as much as we need him at church on Sunday.

That's why in 1999 I started sending out a short e-mail prayer every Monday morning. I sensed that all of us could use some help connecting with God as we went back to the office, school, factory, store, restaurant, or farm. I was a novice with e-mail back then, but this convenient communication tool gave me the chance to offer some encouragement to the dozens of staff members of East 91st Street Christian Church in Indianapolis, where I served as senior minister. When I became president of Cincinnati Christian University in 2002, I continued to e-mail Monday morning prayers to our faculty and staff, and to a growing number of business associates and other friends who requested them.

This book contains 52 of those prayers—one for each week of the year—along with additional prayers for special seasons and holidays. I hope these honest conversations with God

> The God who created the universe
> is also the Lord of Monday morning.

will help you recognize that you are not alone as you start your work-week. The God who created the universe is also the Lord of Monday morning.

I hope these prayers will lighten your load, encourage your heart, and lift your eyes to loftier things than the stack of "to do" items waiting for you at work.

The Bible says, "Let us then approach the throne of grace with confidence, so that we may receive mercy and find grace to help us in our time of need" (Hebrews 4:16). I can't think of a better way to start a Monday morning. ♨

David Faust
President
Cincinnati Christian University

Prayers to Start the Work-Week

1. AMBITION

"I press on toward the goal" (Philippians 3:14).

Lord,

I want the faith of Abraham, to trust you for blessings beyond my imagination.

I want the vision of Joseph, to see your hand at work even in difficult circumstances.

I want the tenacity of Moses, to persevere toward the Promised Land even if it takes years to get there.

I want the boldness of Joshua, to fight the good fight of faith.

And that's not all.

I want the worshipful heart of David,
      The wisdom of Solomon,
      The fortitude of Daniel,
      The compassion of Jeremiah,
      The courage of Esther,

Help me to fight the good fight of faith.

      The faithfulness of Mary,
      The adventurous spirit of Peter,
      The missionary zeal of Paul,
      The encouraging attitude of Barnabas,
      The loving spirit of John.

So that you will see these character qualities in me, O Lord, I want to imitate these heroic examples described in your Word.

And yet . . .
I can only be myself.

So help me this week, Lord, to be my best self—growing more and more like the greatest example of all, Jesus Christ. In his name I pray. Amen. ⚱

2. ATTITUDE

"Your attitude should be the same as that of Christ Jesus"
(Philippians 2:5).

Father in Heaven,

How easy it is to have a bad attitude—and how important to have a good one! I cannot be a leader at home or at work unless my own attitude is right. Before I can influence others, first I need you to shape my own perspective and mold my character as you see fit.

Make me fair. Help me to deal justly and honorably with others this week.

Make me brave. Give me the courage to raise issues that need to be addressed, to speak up for what is right, and to confront what needs to be corrected.

Make me daring, willing to attempt what I can achieve only by faith.

Make me wise. Help me to "hate what is evil" and "cling to what is good" (Romans 12:9). Give me the discernment to make good decisions.

Make me positive. Remove from my heart any tendency to grumble, complain, or grow bitter. Teach me to be content. Help me never to

Don't let me be satisfied with mediocrity.

miss an opportunity to encourage someone who needs it. Restore the joy of my salvation and the excitement of making a difference.

Make me pure. Scrub away the sin that tarnishes my heart and hinders my witness for you. Protect me from Satan's attacks. Strengthen me to win the battle when sinful desires war against my soul.

Make me effective. Spur me on toward excellence in my work. Don't let me be satisfied with mediocrity or a half-hearted effort. Enable me to accomplish the mission you have set before me.

Guard my mind, Lord. This week let my attitude reflect the holy mind of Christ, in whose name I pray. Amen. ☕

3. AWE

". . . Since we are receiving a kingdom that cannot be shaken, let us be thankful, and so worship God acceptably with reverence and awe" (Hebrews 12:28).

"Therefore stand in awe of God" (Ecclesiastes 5:7).

Lord God,

Awesome has become an overused and empty word—but not when I think of you.

I stand in awe of your creative power when thunder rumbles in the sky, when snow blows in the wind, and when flowers spring up from the ground. I am amazed at your creativity when I visit the zoo, when I gaze at the mountains, and when I stand on the beach looking at the vast ocean.

I stand in awe of your wisdom when I read the Bible, and words you guided men to write in Scripture thousands of years ago speak directly to my needs today.

I stand in awe of your creative power.

I stand in awe of your artistry when I hear a stirring song, eat a delicious meal, or see a baby smile.

I stand in awe of your grandeur when I look at the stars on a clear summer night and realize the universe is bigger than I can comprehend, and when I meet friends from other nations and catch a glimpse of the global scope of your love for every person and every ethnic group on earth.

I stand in awe of your grace when I realize how flawed I am. How merciful you are to consider me your friend, your child, your coworker!

I stand in awe of your faithfulness when I think about how you have taken care of me throughout my life, in spite of all my worries and cares.

Throughout the coming week, I will stand in awe of you, O God. Through Christ the Lord I pray. Amen. ☙

4. BUDGET

"Azmaveth son of Adiel was in charge of the royal storehouses. . . . Ezri son of Kelub was in charge of the field workers who farmed the land. Shimei the Ramathite was in charge of the vineyards for the wine vats . . . . Joash was in charge of the supplies of olive oil. . . . Obil the Ishmaelite was in charge of the camels. Jehdeiah the Meronothite was in charge of the donkeys. Jaziz the Hagrite was in charge of the flocks. All these were the officials in charge of King David's property" (1 Chronicles 27:25-31).

"Whoever can be trusted with very little can also be trusted with much, and whoever is dishonest with very little will also be dishonest with much. So if you have not been trustworthy in handling worldly wealth, who will trust you with true riches? And if you have not been trustworthy with someone else's property, who will give you property of your own?" (Luke 16:10-12).

Lord God,

Numbers aren't my favorite thing, but they're a necessary thing. Dollars aren't an evil thing, but they're a dangerous thing. Budgets aren't the main thing that should consume my time, but without them my resources will be consumed by the wrong things.

Just as David put trustworthy servants in charge of his property, you have trusted me with responsibility for the financial wellbeing of my family and my colleagues at work. If Obil could

I want to be faithful with everything you have trusted to my care.

take care of the camels and Jehdeiah could take care of the donkeys, surely with your help I can take care of the line-items on my budget.

So make me a wise steward of my personal finances and of the budget entrusted to me at work. Keep my motives pure, my mind sharp, my calculations accurate, and my ethics completely honest and above board. Surround me with wise financial advisors and keep my mind open to their counsel. Protect me from foolish mistakes that would misuse or squander any of the resources you have provided.

In financial matters, show me the right balance between boldness and timidity, between excessive risk and unnecessary caution. Help me to spend carefully, invest wisely, save diligently, give generously, and plan prudently. Free me from the love of money, which is "a root of all kinds of evil" (1 Timothy 6:10). Protect me from every form of "greed, which is idolatry" (Colossians 3:5). Help me to be fair in the way I pay others for their work, just as I want others to treat me when I'm on the receiving end of the paycheck.

You are the owner and I am the caretaker of your property. I want to be faithful with everything you have trusted to my care. Make me a faithful steward, O Lord. I pray this in the name of the righteous Son of God. Amen.

5. BURDENS

"Cast all your anxiety on him because he cares for you" (1 Peter 5:7).

"Praise be to the Lord, to God our Savior, who daily bears our burdens" (Psalm 68:19).

Father in Heaven,

What a humbling realization—that you bear my burdens every day! You've told me to cast all my anxiety on you, so I cast my burdens on your strong shoulders. And I pray for others around me who need your loving care.

Some carry emotional burdens like discouragement, depression, and sadness. Comfort those who miss loved ones who have died or moved away.

Some carry physical burdens. They live with chronic pain, frustrating disabilities, or wearisome allergies and other illnesses that sap their strength and diminish their joy. I ask for healing, but I also ask for the ability to serve you at maximum strength even when our bodies function at less than 100 percent.

Some carry financial burdens. I trust you, Lord, to provide for every true need. Help your people to be good stewards. Give us

I cast my burdens on your strong shoulders.

wisdom to make the right choices about what we spend, what we give, and what we save. Teach us the secret of contentment.

Some carry family burdens. Lord, I pray for all of my friends and coworkers whose families are a source of frustration instead of joy. I pray for healthy marriages, healthy friendships, and healthy relationships between brothers and sisters, in-laws, children and grandchildren. Please bless these dear ones with your protection and guidance.

Thank you for caring about your people, Lord. This week, give me peace so I can serve you without unnecessary distractions. I cast my burdens on you in the name of Christ, who promised that his burden would be light. Amen.

6. COMFORT

"Blessed are those who mourn, for they will be comforted" (Matthew 5:4).

"Praise be to the God and Father of our Lord Jesus Christ, the Father of compassion and the God of all comfort, who comforts us in all our troubles, so that we can comfort those in any trouble with the comfort we ourselves have received from God" (2 Corinthians 1:3,4).

"We pray you, Master, be our helper and protector. Save those of us in affliction, have mercy on the humble, raise up the fallen, manifest yourself to those in need, heal the sick, bring back those of your people who are straying. Feed the hungry, ransom our prisoners, raise up the weak, comfort the faint-hearted. Let all the nations know you—that you are God alone and Jesus Christ is your Servant and we are your people and the sheep of your pasture. Amen."
—Clement of Rome (AD 30-100)

I praise you, God of all comfort!

In so many hearts today there is an unspoken sadness, an unrelenting ache, a sense of brokenness. Life is filled with losses: lost health, lost friends, lost youth, lost security, lost income, lost idealism. Some around me today are mourning because they miss loved ones who have died; make me sensitive to their hurts. Others I will encounter today grieve because of unrealized dreams and unfulfilled expectations; use me to renew their hope.

I must be willing to mourn, Lord. Let me taste the sadness you feel because there's so much sin and hurt in this mixed-up world. Touch my heart with grief for children who have been

"Weeping may remain for a night, but rejoicing comes in the morning" (Psalm 30:5).

physically, emotionally, or sexually abused. Stir my compassion for the masses who live under cruel dictatorships, oppressive Islamic regimes, and atheistic Communism. Let me never forget the pain of those who live in nations where their leaders build bombs while their people face poverty and starvation.

➤

Burden my heart for the throngs who have never heard the gospel and for the multitudes in my own nation who have heard it but act as if it's irrelevant. Let me never grow complacent and uncaring when I hear about broken families, divided churches, and leaders who experience moral failure.

At the same time, Lord, I thank you for the assurance that "weeping may remain for a night, but rejoicing comes in the morning" (Psalm 30:5). Thank you for the comforting presence of your Holy Spirit, the greatest Comforter. Thank you for your promises written in Scripture. Thank you for the hope of eternal life, guaranteed by the resurrection of Jesus Christ. Thank you that my labors are not in vain.

I take comfort, Lord, in your love. Enable me to comfort others this week. In the name of Christ. Amen. ☕

7. COMMUNITY

". . . Love your neighbor as yourself" (Leviticus 19:18).

"Seek the peace and prosperity of the city . . . . Pray to the Lord for it, because if it prospers, you too will prosper" (Jeremiah 29:7).

Lord God,

Long ago you instructed the Jewish people who had been carried into exile in Babylon not to be discouraged even though their city was filled with spiritual danger.

Today I pray for my community. I pray that all who live here will sense your presence in our neighborhood as we work, shop, drive, play, and worship.

I pray for those who lead our city's churches and schools, for law enforcement officials and those involved in local government. I pray for teachers and business leaders and for all who labor in factories, stores, gas stations, and restaurants. I pray for bus drivers and truck drivers, those who repair the

Make me a vessel of righteousness, respect, and peace as I interact with my neighbors.

highways, those who work in hospitals and clinics, and those who grow and sell our food. I pray for the children and teens who play in the parks and walk the streets at night. I pray for those who are sick, those who are in prison, and those who have no faith in Christ.

Make me a vessel of righteousness, respect, and peace as I interact with my neighbors, and help me to remember that all of these neighbors are precious to you. Bring an end to the racial strife in my city, and purge me from any sinful remnants of prejudice I harbor in my heart. Make me sensitive to the needs of those around me, and give me opportunities to share the good news of Christ.

This week let me seek the peace and prosperity of my city, Lord God, so that your name will be glorified here—and to the ends of the earth. I pray in the name of Jesus, who wept over the city of Jerusalem. Amen. ☙

8. COMPASSION

"When he saw the crowds, he had compassion on them, because they were harassed and helpless, like sheep without a shepherd" (Matthew 9:36).

I confess, Father,

that I don't always see crowds that way. People get in my way. They make demands of me. Crowded highways slow me down. Personality clashes irritate and annoy me. Many of my neighbors simply keep to themselves, and I don't know how to approach them.

But Lord, you have called me to be different. You have called me to care. Give me a heart of compassion. As Jesus did, let me see the real condition of my neighbors' hearts. So many are

Open my eyes to the needs of my neighborhood, my city, and my world.

harassed and helpless, and they don't know where to turn for help. On the outside some appear to have it all together, but the reality is, they desperately need you. Others seem so far gone, so hardened by sin, that it's hard to imagine they would ever accept Christ.

Remind me that the gospel is the power of God for salvation. Keep alive in me a deep appreciation for your grace. Fan into flame my desire to share your good news by word and by deed. Open my eyes to the needs of my neighborhood, my city, and my world. Help me to cross racial, cultural, and generational barriers with your love. Show me how to build healthy relationships with my neighbors and coworkers. Give me opportunities to gently and respectfully explain the reason for the hope in my heart (1 Peter 3:15).

Let me never forget that if you were not my shepherd, I would be lost, too.

I pray in the name of the Good Shepherd who is always on the alert for lost sheep. Amen. ☕

9. CONFLICT

"Blessed are the peacemakers, for they will be called sons of God. Blessed are those who are persecuted because of righteousness, for theirs is the kingdom of heaven. Blessed are you when people insult you, persecute you and falsely say all kinds of evil against you because of me. Rejoice and be glad, because great is your reward in heaven, for in the same way they persecuted the prophets who were before you" (Matthew 5:9-12).

Great and Mighty God, Defender of the Weak and Powerless,

There is so little peace on earth.

As war continues to plague the nations of the world, I lift up to you the leaders of governments and armies. Grant them wisdom and good judgment. Give them the right balance of courage and restraint. I pray for the soldiers who lay their lives on the line, and for their families who await their homecomings with pride and concern.

Help me to remember, Lord, that you are the ultimate in homeland security. You are the author of freedom, the forgiver of

Guide me to be an agent of reconciliation, a force for peace.

sin, the protector of children, and the encourager of the old. You are the rising sun of hope after the dark night of despair.

You are the avenger of wrong, the guardian of right, and the healer of the broken. You are "the God of peace" (Romans 16:20). Your Son Jesus is the "Prince of Peace" (Isaiah 9:6). Your Holy Spirit, the Comforter, has come to bring peace (John 14:26, 27).

This week, help me to be a peacemaker, too—not just a peacekeeper. Restore any broken relationships in my life that need your healing hand. Give me the courage to confront and resolve the conflicts I face at home and at work. Guide me to be an agent of reconciliation, a force for peace.

➤

➤

Please protect and strengthen my brothers and sisters throughout the world who are facing conflict and persecution because of their faith. I pray for believers who struggle to proclaim the gospel in the Middle East, and in North Korea, China, India, Sudan, Cuba, and Indonesia. I pray for Christian leaders in Eastern Europe, who still labor to overcome the darkness created by years of atheism and harsh rule in their homelands.

Forgive me, Lord, for magnifying my own troubles while lacking concern for my suffering sisters and brothers. Keep alive in me a strong sense of compassion for "those in prison" and "those who are mistreated" (Hebrews 13:3). Forgive me for taking for granted the freedom to worship, assemble, and speak out that I enjoy in America.

And help me to endure those moments when I myself might be criticized, misunderstood, slandered, and mistreated because of my faith. In my times of personal conflict and loneliness, be my friend and guide—a "very present help in times of trouble" (Psalm 46:1, *King James Version*).

I pray in the name of the Prince of Peace. Amen. ☕

10. COURAGE

"Be strong and very courageous. Be careful to obey all the law my servant Moses gave you; do not turn from it to the right or to the left, that you may be successful wherever you go" (Joshua 1:7).

"Be on your guard; stand firm in the faith; be men of courage; be strong" (1 Corinthians 16:13).

"For it is God's will that by doing good you should silence the ignorant talk of foolish men" (1 Peter 2:15).

Enemies of the cross are making noise, Lord.
> Silence them.

Gossips and slanderers are tearing your church apart.
> Silence them.

Purveyors of pornography are polluting minds with impure thoughts.
> Silence them.

Doubts assail your people and threaten to drown out the song of faith.
> Silence them.

Do not let me be overwhelmed by fear.

But there are other sounds, Lord.

Your people are singing your praises.
> Amplify them.

Your messengers are preaching your truth.
> Strengthen them.

Your servants are taking the gospel to the ends of the earth.
> Go with them and make them bold.

And make me bold, Lord.

Make me like Abraham and Sarah, who had the courage to follow even though they didn't know where you were leading them.

Make me like Joseph, who had the moral courage to say "no" to Potiphar's wife and trust in you even when doing the right thing landed him in jail.

➤

Make me like Moses, who boldly stood up to Pharaoh when you ordered, "Let my people go."

Make me like Joshua, who courageously led his army into battle.

Make me like Caleb, who had the fortitude to say, "Give me this mountain" and tackle a tough military assignment when he was already in his 80s.

Make me like David, who was willing to challenge Goliath.

Make me like the prophets Nathan, Elijah, Isaiah, and Daniel, who had the courage to confront kings even when they had to tell them bad news.

Make me like John the Baptist, who had the courage to tell King Herod it was wrong for him to commit adultery.

Make me like Jesus, who had the courage to rebuke the Pharisees, challenge longstanding traditions, and reach out and touch people with the contagious skin disease of leprosy.

Make me like the apostle Paul, who showed incredible courage when he traveled the Mediterranean as a missionary.

Lord, my very best decisions have been the times when I have chosen to walk by faith, not by sight—to take risks instead of playing it safe. Do not let me be overwhelmed by fear. Give me clarity to know what I ought to do, and give me the courage to do it. This is my prayer in the strong name of Jesus, who "resolutely set out for Jerusalem" (Luke 9:51) even though he knew the cross awaited him there. Amen. ☕

11. EMPATHY

"Do nothing out of selfish ambition or vain conceit, but in humility consider others better than yourselves. Each of you should look not only to your own interests, but also to the interests of others" (Philippians 2:3, 4).

Dear Lord,

Francis of Assisi prayed, "O divine Master, grant that I may not so much seek to be consoled as to console; to be understood as to understand; to be loved as to love." I want to be aware of and sensitive to the thoughts, feelings, and experiences of others. But how can I understand what I never have personally experienced?

I have experienced neither impressive wealth nor oppressive poverty, so how can I relate to the temptations of the rich or the deprivations of the destitute? I've never been imprisoned, so how can I apply the verse that says, "Remember those in prison as if you were their fellow prisoners, and those who are mistreated as if you yourselves were suffering" (Hebrews 13:3)?

Empathy is hard work. Assist me, Lord, to polish up my personal paradigms. Every day I encounter those who look at

Lord, help me to understand others around me.

life through a very different lens than my own. If I don't keep my own values and convictions sharp, how can I help anyone else?

Help me not to pre-judge, but to pre-love. This week make me an ambassador of grace and truth, treating everyone I meet "with gentleness and respect" (1 Peter 3:15). Even when I don't see eye-to-eye with others, help us relate heart-to-heart.

Help me, Lord, to talk less and listen more. Let me ask thoughtful questions and pay careful attention to the answers. "The purposes of a man's heart are deep waters, but a man of understanding draws them out" (Proverbs 20:5).

And help me to put myself in the place of others. If I can't walk a mile in their shoes, let me at least try them on for size.

Lord, help me to understand others around me. Some people are hurting today. Be their counselor, the one who gives them comfort. Some of my coworkers are tired today. Refresh them even as they work, and give them rest when the day comes to an end. Some feel frustrated and worried today. Quiet their hearts and give them peace.

This is my prayer in the name of Christ, the great empathizer, who knows firsthand the pain of loneliness, the sorrow of grief, the joy of accomplishment, the sting of betrayal, and the power of redemption. Amen.

12. EXCELLENCE

". . . That you may live a life worthy of the Lord and may please him in every way, bearing fruit in every good work, growing in the knowledge of God" (Colossians 1:10).

How excellent is your name, O Lord!

You have said in your Word that "if anything is excellent or praiseworthy," I should "think about such things" (Philippians 4:8). So help me, Lord, to honor you with excellence this week.

You have said that "we are God's workmanship, created in Christ Jesus to do good works, which God prepared in advance

Stir in me a holy dissatisfaction with the status quo.

for us to do" (Ephesians 2:10). I am saved by your grace, not by my own works; but I am saved to do good works that will honor your name and reflect my love for you.

Stir in me a holy dissatisfaction with the status quo so I will keep striving to improve things around me and make them better—not to impress others, but simply because you deserve nothing less than my best.

Lord, this week make me diligent in my work, giving my best effort in everything I do. This is my prayer and my promise in the powerful name of Jesus, the ultimate example of excellence in word and deed. Amen. ♨

13. FAITH (I)

"Now to him who is able to do immeasurably more than all we ask or imagine, according to his power that is at work within us, to him be glory in the church and in Christ Jesus throughout all generations, forever and ever! Amen" (Ephesians 3:20, 21).

Lord God,

You are calling me to go beyond my comfort zone. Beyond where I've been before. Beyond what I assume is possible.

You called Abraham to follow you to a strange new land. You led Moses to guide his people out of slavery and into the land of milk and honey. You changed a young shepherd into King David. You transformed humble fishermen like Peter, Andrew, James and John into world-changing leaders. You called Saul of Tarsus even while he was an enemy of the church, then used him beyond what anyone could have imagined as a spokesman for you.

Put me out on a limb—for that is where the fruit grows.

Lord, I boldly pray that you will increase my faith. Broaden my influence. Take me to new levels of impact for the glory of your name.

Forgive my small thinking and my moments of pessimism and unbelief. Keep my dreams alive and make them big, inspiring, and achievable. Open new doors of opportunity for me to make a difference. Move me beyond the limitations of my human weaknesses and into your power, which makes all things possible.

In these times of economic anxiety, there's no recession in your care. In these times of fear, faith is still the victory that overcomes the world. In these times of uncertainty, you are still the unchanging bedrock on which wise builders construct our lives.

Increase my faith, Lord. Put me out on a limb—for that is where the fruit grows. In Jesus' name. Amen. ☕

14. FAITH (II)

"Behold, Lord, an empty vessel that needs to be filled.
My Lord, fill it.
I am weak in the faith;
Strengthen Thou me.
I am cold in love;
Warm me and make me fervent
So that my love may go out to my neighbor.
I do not have a strong and firm faith;
At times I doubt and am unable to trust Thee altogether.
O Lord, help me.
Strengthen my faith and trust in Thee."
—Martin Luther, 1483-1546

"Some trust in chariots and some in horses, but we trust in
the name of the Lord our God" (Psalm 20:7).

Lord God,

I'm not strong enough to handle all of my responsibilities
without your help. Today, please give me strength.

I'm not smart enough to make excellent decisions without your
assistance. Today, please give me wisdom.

All things work together for the good
of those who love you (Romans 8:28).

I'm not talented enough to do my job without relying on your
empowerment. Today, please fill me with your Spirit.

Lord, I'm not aware enough of others' hurts, viewpoints, and
motives to fully understand those around me. Please give me
patience with everyone I encounter today, and help me to see
them through your eyes.

➤

I'm not visionary enough to see the big picture—how you are constantly providing for me, stretching me, using me for your purposes, and causing all things to work together for the good of those who love you (Romans 8:28). Today, may my faith grow stronger and my dreams grow bigger.

Father, I believe in you. This week I will rely on you. I pray in the name of the one who said that faith can move mountains. Amen. ☕

15. FAMILY

". . . Each one of you must love his wife as he loves himself, and the wife must respect her husband. Children, obey your parents in the Lord, for this is right. 'Honor your father and mother.' . . . Fathers, do not exasperate your children; instead, bring them up in the training and instruction of the Lord"
(Ephesians 5:33-6:4).

Father in Heaven,

I pray for my family, Lord. Remind me that "love your neighbor" means meeting the needs of my closest neighbors—those who live in my own home.

Help me to be the kind of spouse you want me to be. Strengthen my marriage. Deepen my love for my spouse. Enable us to communicate openly, to forgive freely, and to be faithful always. Help me to win my ongoing battle with selfishness.

I pray for my children and grandchildren. Build up their faith. Let me teach them well, by word and by deed. Give me grace

Put my household on the path to wholeness and holiness.

to release the next generation into your care instead of holding onto them too tightly. I pray for their physical, relational, and emotional health. Encourage them when they feel disheartened and overwhelmed. Strengthen their bodies through exercise, rest, and nourishing food. Deliver them from harmful habits and dangerous people. Comfort them when they face the difficult situations life is sure to bring their way. Keep them safe as they travel. Surround them with good friends and with people they can serve in Jesus' name. O Lord, steel them against temptation. Burn your Word deeply into their hearts. Help them to sense your guiding presence. Stir in them a deep and abiding awareness of the great value you place on their lives.

Help me to honor my parents and grandparents and repay them for the love they have shown to me.

➤

And Lord, wherever there is dysfunction and brokenness in my family, help me to be a source of healing instead of adding further pain or confusion. Put my household on the path to wholeness and holiness.

I offer this prayer in the name of Jesus, who made it clear that his true family consists of all who do the will of God (Mark 3:35). Amen.

16. FOCUS

"But one thing I do: Forgetting what is behind and straining toward what is ahead, I press on toward the goal . . ." (Philippians 3:13, 14).

Father in Heaven,

My life is complicated. Grant me discernment so I can sift through the confusion.

My life is busy. Guide me to find time for the things you consider most important.

My life is passing quickly. Enable me to see each day as an investment in eternity.

My life is sometimes painful. Give me strength to endure hardship and to bear others' burdens along with my own.

My life is interwoven with the lives of others. Break me out of my self-made shell, and help me to reach out to my neighbors with selflessness and love.

My life matters. Keep me from wasting precious hours doubting my worth or questioning the significance of my efforts.

Each day is an investment in eternity.

My life is filled with blessings. Give me a grateful heart and eyes to see your hand at work in all the good things I enjoy.

My life is your gift. Thank you, Lord, for each new day, each breath of air, each beat of my heart, and each friend you bring across my path.

This week, keep my eyes fixed on the goal. I pray in the name of Jesus, who fulfilled his purpose even when it meant going to the cross. Amen.

17. FORGIVENESS (I)

"Forgive us our debts, as we also have forgiven our debtors" (Matthew 6:12).

"If we confess our sins, he is faithful and just and will forgive us our sins and purify us from all unrighteousness" (1 John 1:9).

Gracious God,

How great is your mercy! How vast is your ocean of forgiveness! How intense was the suffering of Christ so that I could be pardoned and redeemed! Thank you, Father, for the promises in your Word that assure me of your willingness to forgive.

"If you, O Lord, kept a record of sins, O Lord, who could stand? But with you there is forgiveness; therefore you are feared" (Psalm 130:3, 4).

"You will again have compassion on us; you will tread our sins underfoot and hurl all our iniquities into the depths of the sea" (Micah 7:19).

Help me to keep a clean slate with those around me.

Show me how to grant mercy toward others, Lord. Help me to keep a clean slate with those around me—no resentment, no unfair judgment of motives, no seeds of bitterness taking root in my heart.

I have received your amazing grace, Lord. This week let me show it to everyone I meet.

I pray in the name of Christ, who even prayed for the forgiveness of those who nailed him to the cross. Amen. ☕

18. FORGIVENESS (II)

"Do not repay anyone evil for evil. Be careful to do what is right in the eyes of everybody. If it is possible, as far as it depends on you, live at peace with everyone. . . . Do not be overcome by evil, but overcome evil with good"
(Romans 12:17-21).

Father,

From a human perspective, sometimes it's not possible to be reconciled with everyone. But if it is possible (and usually it is), as far as it depends on me (and frequently it does), help me to be at peace with others.

If I have failed to act with love, forgive me.

If I have hurt anyone—intentionally or unintentionally—heal the wounds and give both of us strength to try again.

If I am still hanging onto any old grievances I should have released long ago, please cut them loose.

If barriers of hostility or mistrust are shutting me off from my brothers and sisters, remove them and repair the bonds of fellowship.

Help me to "overcome evil with good."

If in the process of doing my job I have forgotten to treat my coworkers with respect and dignity, forgive me and help me not to repeat that mistake.

Take me to a new and better level in my relationships with others, Lord. Help me to "overcome evil with good." I pray in the name of Jesus, who suffered though he didn't deserve it, so that those who don't deserve forgiveness can receive it. Amen. ☕

19. GENEROSITY

"A generous man will prosper; he who refreshes others will himself be refreshed" (Proverbs 11:25).

"Each man should give what he has decided in his heart to give, not reluctantly or under compulsion, for God loves a cheerful giver. And God is able to make all grace abound to you, so that in all things at all times, having all that you need, you will abound in every good work" (2 Corinthians 9:7, 8).

Lord,

Make me generous.

Make me generous with my words, encouraging and uplifting others around me with sincere words of appreciation and praise. Let me practice the teaching of Hebrews 3:13, which says to "encourage one another daily."

Make me generous with my deeds, going the extra mile in my daily work and my service to others. Remind me that

> You love a cheerful giver because you ARE a cheerful giver.

one reason you have given me a job is so that I "may have something to share with those in need" (Ephesians 4:28).

Show me how to be generous with my money—never stingy, not holding back, but honoring you faithfully with my tithes and offerings. May I always give out of a heart that overflows with love for you and your people. Remind me, Lord, that you love a cheerful giver because you ARE a cheerful giver. Help me to "excel in this grace of giving" (2 Corinthians 8:7).

Make me generous and gracious in my attitude—not hyper-critical or given to harsh judgment. May I fulfill the Scriptural admonition that says, "Accept one another, then, just as Christ accepted you, in order to bring praise to God" (Romans 15:7).

You are a generous and gracious God, the giver of "every good and perfect gift" (James 1:17). May my life reflect your generosity this week. I offer this prayer in the name of Jesus, the most generous and other-centered person who ever walked the earth. Amen. ☕

"Even though I walk through the valley of the shadow of death, I will fear no evil, for you are with me; your rod and your staff, they comfort me" (Psalm 23:4).

"Brothers, we do not want you to be ignorant about those who fall asleep, or to grieve like the rest of men, who have no hope" (1 Thessalonians 4:13).

Living God, Giver of Comfort and Life,

Bless all of my loved ones who currently walk through the valley of the shadow of death.

For friends who grieve the death of a loved one (whether their loved one died days ago or years ago), I ask you to comfort them and replace their emptiness with hope.

For all who face serious illness or impending death, please provide an extra measure of your healing grace.

For those whose loved ones travel the highways, live in dangerous areas, or work in hazardous occupations, and for those who work in public safety and military service, I pray for your protection to surround them.

For all who find themselves traveling through the death-like valley of loneliness and depression, please give them the gift

Thank you for leading me through the dark valleys.

of friendship and encouragement, and fill them with a keen awareness of your presence.

For all who feel afraid, give them courage, strength, and boldness to live by faith.

No matter what dark shadows I personally face today, keep me walking in the light of your Word. Use your rod of discipline and your staff of protection to nudge me in the right direction. Remind me that my biggest problem has already been solved, for through the death and resurrection of Jesus you have removed the sting of death and replaced it with eternal life.

Because of you, God, I will fear no evil. Thank you for leading me through the dark valleys. I pray in the name of the living Christ, who is the Light of the world. Amen. ☙

21. GROWTH

"Love the Lord your God with all your heart and with all your soul and with all your mind and with all your strength" (Mark 12:30).

"For this very reason, make every effort to add to your faith goodness; and to goodness, knowledge; and to knowledge, self-control; and to self-control, perseverance; and to perseverance, godliness; and to godliness, brotherly kindness; and to brotherly kindness, love. For if you possess these qualities in increasing measure, they will keep you from being ineffective and unproductive in your knowledge of our Lord Jesus Christ"
(2 Peter 1:5-8).

Father,

What would happen if I loved you more today than I did yesterday? What would happen if I stopped holding back and quit giving you only a portion of my devotion?

What if, because I love you, I put even ten percent more effort into my work? More brain-power into my worship? More

I give you my whole heart, mind, soul, and strength.

diligence into my study? More enthusiasm into my service to others?

What if, because I love you, I would make it my goal to bear maximum fruit for you today?

Lord God, help me to love you fully—without holding anything back. Help me to grow in faith, goodness, knowledge, self-control, perseverance, godliness, brotherly kindness, and love. This week I give you my whole heart, mind, soul, and strength. This is my prayer in the name of Christ, who on the cross sacrificed every part of himself without holding anything back. Amen. ☕

22. GUIDANCE

"For having many friends cannot benefit, strong helpers cannot assist, wise counselors cannot give a beneficial answer, books written by knowledgeable people cannot comfort, valuable items cannot deliver, and no matter how lovely a place is it cannot shelter—unless you yourself assist, help, strengthen, comfort, instruct, and guard us. . . . I look, therefore, to you my God, the Father of mercies, and in you I put my trust."
—Thomas a Kempis

"Trust in the Lord with all your heart and lean not on your own understanding; in all your ways acknowledge him, and he will direct your paths" (Proverbs 3:5, 6).

Father in Heaven,

When I walk down a rocky and dangerous path, you show me the way. Lord, be my guide.

When I feel worried and confused, you hold things together. Lord, be my peace.

When I'm tempted to be lazy and apathetic, you spur me on. Lord, be my motivator, my inspiration, my coach.

*If I lean on my own understanding,
I will surely go astray.*

When I'm selfish, you compel me to care about others. Lord, be my example of love.

When I'm afraid, you are my bold and fearless leader. Lord, be my protector and my source of courage.

When death and darkness threaten to overwhelm me, you give me strength to carry on. Lord, be my comfort, my encourager, my hope-giver.

When darkness closes in, you show me the way. Lord, be my light.

If I lean on my own understanding, I will surely go astray. So guide me, Lord, and direct my paths this week. This is my prayer in the name of Jesus, who told his disciples, "Come, follow me." Amen. ☕

23. HUMILITY

"He has showed you, O man, what is good. And what does the Lord require of you? To act justly and to love mercy and to walk humbly with your God" (Micah 6:8).

"Blessed are the poor in spirit, for theirs is the kingdom of heaven. . . . Blessed are the meek, for they will inherit the earth" (Matthew 5:3, 5).

Father,

It's hard to understand what it means to be "poor in spirit." I'm surrounded by a culture that teaches me to be self-sufficient, to act like I'm in control—on top of things. It goes against my pride to think that the pathway of blessing requires utter dependence on you.

Forgive me for relying on my own knowledge and ability instead of yours. Help me always to remember that you have infinitely more experience than I do. Teach me the hard lessons of

Only when I am truly poor in spirit will I discover the wonderful riches you have for me in Christ.

humility and meekness, for only when I am truly poor in spirit will I discover the wonderful riches you have for me in Christ.

I know from your Word that meekness is not just being passive and "nice." It's not just taking the safe route and avoiding risk at any cost. Give me the kind of meekness I see in strong leaders like Moses, David, Paul—and most of all in Jesus, who was loving and kind, but also firm.

Help me, Father, to be strong in my core convictions but gentle as I deal with people. Make me firm in my faith but flexible in matters of opinion. Give me the boldness to speak up whenever needed, and the wisdom to keep my mouth shut when silence is the better choice. Let me submit to authority with proper respect and be patient when I don't get my own way.

This week, make me meek. I pray in the name of the one who humbled himself and became a servant, obeying your will even to the point of death on the cross. Amen. ☕

24. INTEGRITY

"Search me, O God, and know my heart; test me and know my anxious thoughts. See if there is any offensive way in me, and lead me in the way everlasting" (Psalm 139:23, 24).

"In everything set them an example by doing what is good. In your teaching show integrity, seriousness and soundness of speech that cannot be condemned . . ." (Titus 2:7, 8).

*"From the cowardice that dare not face new truth,
From the laziness that is contented with half truth,
From the arrogance that thinks it knows all truth,
Good Lord, deliver me."
—A Kenyan prayer (author unknown)*

God of holiness and truth,

You know my heart better than anyone else. Make me a person of integrity.

Your truth shines like a searchlight on my inmost being. You know my motives, my anxious thoughts, my worries and fears. You know how I act, what I say, what I feel—and why.

Lord, purge from my life anything that's offensive to you. Make me the real deal, authentic and genuine. Take away any hint of hypocrisy from my heart. Make me honest in my words, genuine

Leadership is not an image to be created; it's a character to be developed.

in my faith, straightforward and trustworthy in my dealings with others. Make my actions line up with my beliefs, my attitude align with the values I profess.

Free me from phoniness and game-playing. Keep me from bending the truth or compromising my convictions. Remind me that leadership is not an image to be created; it's a character to be developed. Ministry is not an impression to make; it's a mission to carry out.

➤

May my words be true.
May my faith be real.
May my motives be pure.
May my enthusiasm be genuine.
May my love for you be authentic.

Help me to conduct myself with the highest standards of honesty in the way I deal with my family and friends, my finances, my coworkers and business partners. Help me to represent your own integrity with sincerity and authenticity. Help me this week to be completely honest with you, with myself, and with everyone else I encounter.

Make me a person of integrity, Lord. I ask this in the strong name of Jesus Christ, who always spoke the truth in love. Amen.

25. LOVE

"[Love] is not rude, it is not self-seeking, it is not easily angered . . . . Love never fails. . . . When I was a child, I talked like a child, I thought like a child, I reasoned like a child. When I became a man, I put childish ways behind me" (1 Corinthians 13:5, 8-11).

Father,

Love never fails, but sometimes I fail to love. And when I fail to love, I am incomplete and immature—childish. Move me toward maturity, Lord. Toughen my spiritual muscles. Fill me with the kind of love described in First Corinthians 13.

"Love is not rude," but sometimes I have been. Help me to mind my manners. Forgive me for the times when I have been disrespectful and rude toward my coworkers and less than gracious toward my family and my neighbors. Forgive me for the times when I've been polite on the surface while secretly uttering sarcastic comments under my breath.

"Love is not self-seeking," but sometimes I have been. Forgive me for caring more about my own agenda and reputation than I do about yours. Help me to put others ahead of myself.

"Love is not easily angered," but sometimes I have been. Forgive me for being quick-tempered, irritable, moody, and quick

"All men will know that you are my disciples if you love one another" (John 13:35).

to assign blame. Teach me how to be angry without sinning (Ephesians 4:26). Help me to handle my anger in a healthy, Christ-like way.

Because "love does not envy," free me from territorial rivalries and petty jealousy.

Because "love does not boast and is not proud," forgive me for acting like I know all the answers. Prevent me from becoming arrogant or pursuing personal glory.

➤

Because "love keeps no record of wrongs," snuff out any smoldering embers of resentment and heal any old wounds that have left scars on my heart. Strip away the lingering suspicions and relational barriers that sometimes hover over your people like a heavy fog.

Because "love always protects, always trusts, always hopes, and always perseveres," give me strength to go the extra mile and to never give up.

Father, fill me with your love. I pray in the name of Christ, who said, "All men will know that you are my disciples if you love one another" (John 13:35). Amen. ☕

26. MERCY

"Blessed are the merciful, for they will be shown mercy" (Matthew 5:7).

"Religion that God our Father accepts as pure and faultless is this: to look after orphans and widows in their distress and to keep oneself from being polluted by the world" (James 1:27).

Merciful, Gracious Father in Heaven,

In a culture that emphasizes power, possessions, and prestige, guide me to honor the ones our world tends to forget. Show me how to care for the lonely and the powerless, the weak and the weary—those who, like Jesus, are familiar with grief.

Remind me, Lord, that those who appear to wield little power are incredibly important in your eyes. Help me to see children as living portraits of the humility and trust you want from all of us. Remind me to give proper respect to older men and women—especially to those who live alone and who need my emotional support. Let me never get so busy with my job or my hobbies that I neglect to serve orphans and widows.

Lord, show me what it means to be merciful. In my daily work, at times it's my responsibility to be firm and enforce the rules—to assign a failing grade, insist that a bill be paid, confront a sinning

"Be kind and compassionate to one another, forgiving each other, just as in Christ God forgave you" (Ephesians 4:32).

brother or sister, question a poorly-thought-out policy, challenge a bad attitude, or apply some other principle of discipline. In situations like these, help me to be fair and to act with integrity.

At the same time, Lord, please fill my workplace with mercy. Since you've shown so much grace to me, help me to be gracious toward others. Move me to go the extra mile, do the extra kindness, offer the extra measure of understanding, say the extra prayer, bear the extra burden, and take the extra time for others.

Help me to remember the Scripture that says, "be kind and compassionate to one another, forgiving each other, just as in Christ God forgave you" (Ephesians 4:32).

Make me merciful, O Lord. I pray in the name of Jesus, the friend of widows and little children. Amen. 🖐

27. PASSION

"Blessed are those who hunger and thirst for righteousness,
for they will be filled" (Matthew 5:6).

Father in Heaven,

"As the deer pants for streams of water, so my soul pants for you, O God" (Psalm 42:1). And yet, how easy it is to lose that hunger and thirst! Living in a nation filled with so many religious options is like dining in an all-you-can-eat buffet restaurant. I'm surrounded by so much spiritual food, it is tempting to take it for granted.

I don't want to become so stuffed with Scripture that I lose my appetite for it. I don't want to become so accustomed to prayer that I forget how special it is to approach your throne of grace. I don't want to become so familiar with heaven's treasures that I lose the wonder and joy they inspire.

Forgive my apathy and half-heartedness. Spare me from spiritual dullness. Prevent me from becoming like the Pharisees,

I want to serve your purpose in
my generation before I die.

who memorized and systematized their religious rules but in the process lost their love for you and for your people. Instead, make me like a newborn baby who craves "pure spiritual milk" (1 Peter 2:2).

Fill me with the passion of the apostle Paul, who said, "I consider my life worth nothing to me, if only I may finish the race and complete the task the Lord Jesus has given me—the task of testifying to the gospel of God's grace" (Acts 20:24). Remind me this week to practice the Scripture that says, "Never be lacking in zeal, but keep your spiritual fervor, serving the Lord" (Romans 12:11).

Help me to fulfill what Jesus called the greatest commandment: to "love the Lord your God with all your heart and with all your soul and with all your mind and with all your strength" (Mark 12:30). Help me avoid the rebuke Jesus gave a group of half-hearted Christians when he said that he found their half-heartedness nauseating: "Because you are lukewarm—neither hot nor cold—I am about to spit you out of my mouth" (Revelation 3:16).

Keep me fired up, Lord. Keep me passionate and motivated. Keep alive in me the determined desire to make my life count for things that are eternally worthwhile. Show me what's really important in your eyes. Make me care deeply about those things. And let me refuse to worry about anything else.

Show me how to use my "G.O.P."—my Gifts, Opportunities, and Passion—to bear maximum fruit for you.

When I die, let it be said of me what Acts 13:36 says about the death of David: "For when David had served God's purpose in his own generation, he fell asleep." I want to serve your purpose in my generation before I die. This is my passion.

I'm hungry and thirsty for righteousness, Lord. Please fill me up. Amen.

28. PATIENCE

"Be patient, then, brothers, until the Lord's coming. See how the farmer waits for the land to yield its valuable crop and how patient he is for the autumn and spring rains. You too, be patient and stand firm, because the Lord's coming is near" (James 5:7, 8).

Loving God,

In a fast-paced, microwave-ready, instant-message world, teach me to be patient. When I move too fast, slow me down. Help me to persevere when progress comes slowly and wait faithfully when circumstances or personalities rub me the wrong way.

As Paul told Timothy, help me to fulfill my duties "with great patience and careful instruction" (2 Timothy 4:2).

Give me patience with my circumstances. Grant me strength to persevere as I wait for complicated problems to be untangled,

I trust you to bless me the right way, for the right reason, at the right time.

prayers to be answered, financial burdens to be lifted, family conflicts to be resolved, sicknesses to be healed, houses to be sold, skeptical friends to come to faith, and goals to be accomplished.

Give me patience with other people. We all have so many quirks and imperfections that we will never live and work in harmony unless you give us a healthy dose of grace. When others mess up, fill me with mercy. When I mess up, help me to recognize it and accept responsibility for my actions. When there's a problem I need to talk about with someone else, help me to speak the truth in love. When I struggle to understand, help me to trust the good intentions of others and give them the benefit of the doubt.

Your timing is perfect, Father. I trust you to bless me the right way, for the right reason, at the right time. Thank you for being patient with me. I pray in the name of Christ, who demonstrated amazing patience with his disciples. Amen. ☕

29. PERSEVERANCE

"You, O Lord, keep my lamp burning; my God turns my darkness into light. With your help I can advance against a troop; with my God I can scale a wall" (Psalm 18:28, 29).

"Let us not become weary in doing good, for at the proper time we will reap a harvest if we do not give up" (Galatians 6:9).

Father,

One of the hardest temptations I face is discouragement.

You tell me not to grow weary in doing good, but sometimes it would be easier to give up. I grow tired from the daily grind. Tired of problems I can't solve and situations I can't fix. Tired of the work load I carry. Tired of the pressures of my job and the weight of my responsibilities.

Sometimes it would be easier just to give up and flow with the tide instead of swimming against it. Even the church doesn't always live up to its potential, weakened by division and shallow commitment.

Help me to persevere, Lord. Strengthen my body and renew my mind. When the daily grind threatens to wear me down, give me the energy to work with excellence. Keep my thinking clear and my

When no other friends can be found, remind me that friendship with you is enough.

values sharp. Replenish my spirit with Holy Spirit power. Remind me that I can do all things through Christ, who gives me strength (Philippians 4:13).

Fill me daily with fresh courage and determination to do what is right. Provide me with friends who will give me encouragement when I need it. And when no other friends can be found, remind me that friendship with you is enough.

Let no physical, emotional, financial, relational, or spiritual problem block the path of my obedience.

No challenge is too great for you, Lord. So this week, keep me going. Keep me close to you. Keep my lamp burning.

I pray in the holy name of Christ, who said, "I must keep going today and tomorrow and the next day" (Luke 13:33). Amen. ☕

30. PRAISE (I)

"How good it is to sing praises to our God, how pleasant and fitting to praise him!" (Psalm 147:1).

Lord God,

I offer you my praise,
For you are holy and faithful, merciful and mighty, always reliable and trustworthy.
You are my refuge and strength, a very present help in times of trouble.
You are wise, just, and all-knowing—perfect in all your ways.

Through your perfect Law I have learned that your righteous anger burns against sin,
And through your perfect Son I have discovered your grace to forgive.

You deserve my best efforts and my highest allegiance.
Amid all of the activities of this week, I want to offer you the praise and honor you deserve.

I place my life in your hands.

May my life be a living sacrifice, holy and acceptable to you.

In good times and bad,
You are God and you are good.

When things are pleasant and when things are miserable,
When everything is calm and when it looks like everything is falling apart,
When I laugh and when I cry,
        You are God and you are good.

You are my Rock,
        My Faithful Friend,
                My Good Shepherd,
                        My Perfect Leader.

I love you, I trust you, and I place my life in your hands now and for eternity, in the name of Christ. Amen. ☕

31. PRAISE (II)

"Enter his gates with thanksgiving and his courts with praise; give thanks to him and praise his name. For the Lord is good and his love endures forever; his faithfulness continues through all generations" (Psalm 100:4, 5).

Father in Heaven,

I praise you for who you are.
You are the almighty God—a mighty fortress, all-powerful, never changing.

You are holy and just. I hold you in awe because of your righteous anger against sin and injustice.

You are eternal. I struggle to comprehend your timelessness, but I affirm that you are Lord of the past, the present, and the future—the Master of all time and space.

You are gracious. I do not deserve your kindness and mercy.

I stand amazed in your presence.

You are completely and perfectly wise. Your will is flawless; your Word is unmixed with error; your judgments are perfect; your timing is always right.

You are faithful and loving in all your deeds. I stand amazed in your presence, filled with wonder because of your love.

I praise you for what you have done.
Thank you for giving me life . . . for providing my daily bread . . . for giving me family and friends . . . for work that is significant and worthwhile . . . for sustaining me through hardship . . . for giving me hope. You are the giver of every good and perfect gift. Thank you, Father! Amen. ☕

32. PROTECTION

"You are my hiding place; you will protect me from trouble and surround me with songs of deliverance" (Psalm 32:7).

"And the God of all grace, who called you to his eternal glory in Christ, after you have suffered a little while, will himself restore you and make you strong, firm and steadfast" (1 Peter 5:10).

It's a dangerous world, Father,

so I ask for your protection.

Defend me against "the powers of this dark world" (Ephesians 6:12).

Watch over my loved ones. Protect my children and grandchildren from spiritual and emotional harm. Keep them safe as they travel on the streets and highways.

Protect me from cynicism and unbelief, from pessimism and doubt. Help me to remember that in all things you are working for my good.

You are my stronghold, my guardian, my rock.

Help me never to forget that great question of Scripture, "If God is for us, who can be against us?" (Romans 8:31).

Deliver me from materialism—from trying to find security in the almighty dollar instead of the Almighty God.

Guard me against the prideful self-sufficiency that tempts me to think I can handle life on my own without your help.

Gracious God, you are my stronghold, my guardian, my rock. Hold me in the palm of your hand. This is my prayer in the name of Jesus, my shield and defender. Amen. ☕

33. PROVISION

"Give us today our daily bread" (Matthew 6:11).

Father,

I depend upon you for my physical sustenance. You give me strength to wake up each day—strength to see and hear and taste and smell and touch. Let me never take these blessings for granted.

"Give *us*."
Lord, I pray not only for myself but for your extended family: for those in other parts of the world whose needs are greater than my own, for the starving and the weak, for the lonely and the friendless, for those who live each day knowing that unless you provide their daily bread, they will truly have nothing at all. Lord, fill me with compassion for those who face hunger each day. Through missionaries I support, and through my own involvement in ministry, help me to meet the needs of those who hunger for physical bread and those who hunger and thirst for righteousness.

"*This day*."
Not yesterday. You already took care of me then. Not tomorrow. You told me not to worry about it. Just as you provided daily manna for the Israelites as they traveled across the wilderness,

Thank you for meeting my needs today and every day.

give me just what I need for each day—no more, no less. Today, let me "be generous and willing to share" (1 Timothy 6:18), a good steward of what you provide.

"Our daily *bread*."
Not cake—I don't ask for luxuries. I trust you to provide what I really need to survive and thrive. Thank you for the abundance of delicious, nutritious food I enjoy. Keep me grateful for those who prepare and serve my food and who make the dining experience enjoyable. Bless everyone who grows and serves the food I eat. Help me to treat each one with gratitude and respect.

Father, thank you for meeting my needs today and every day. I pray in the holy name of your Son who said, "I am the Bread of Life." Amen.

34. PURITY

"Blessed are the pure in heart, for they will see God" (Matthew 5:8).

Holy, Flawless God,

It's hard to find anything today that's unpolluted by impurity. Like new-fallen snow that quickly turns to mud and slush, as a culture we have taken your good gifts and tainted them with impurity. We have distorted your gift of sexuality and twisted it into a dirty joke. We have laughed at innocence and called it naive. We have winked at immorality and accepted it as normal. Even in the church, too often we have turned our backs on your call to holy living. Unwilling to stand up and stand out, we have taken the easy way and blended in.

Lord, give me the courage to be different, to be Christ-like, to

Help me to walk away from any situation that would compromise my commitment to my spouse or to my Lord.

be filled with your Spirit. Make me truly holy in my heart—not to show off or to impress other people, but simply to honor you. Like Job, let me make "a covenant with my eyes" not to look upon others with lust (Job 31:1).

Protect me from the scourge of pornography. Reinforce my self-control. Keep my relationships pure and above board. Help me to walk away from any situation that would compromise my commitment to my spouse or to my Lord.

With the psalmist David I pray, "Create in me a clean heart, O God, and renew a steadfast spirit within me" (Psalm 51:10). Through Christ I pray. Amen.

35. QUIETNESS

"The Lord said, 'Go out and stand on the mountain in the presence of the Lord, for the Lord is about to pass by.' Then a great and powerful wind tore the mountains apart and shattered the rocks before the Lord, but the Lord was not in the wind. After the wind there was an earthquake, but the Lord was not in the earthquake. After the earthquake came a fire, but the Lord was not in the fire. And after the fire came a gentle whisper"
(1 Kings 19:11, 12).

Father,

In the midst of a noisy culture where all kinds of things clamor for attention, help me to hear your "still, small voice." In the midst of this busy week, help me to find time for silent reflection and prayer.

Don't let me be overly impressed by the loud and the grandiose—the earthquakes and fires where you are not present. Instead, help me to hear your gentle whispers in the words of Scripture and in the wise counsel of godly friends.

Help me to hear your gentle whispers.

As John G. Whittier wrote, "Drop Thy still dews of quietness till all our strivings cease. Take from our souls the strain and stress, and let our ordered lives confess the beauty of Thy peace."

I pray in the name of Christ, who "often withdrew to lonely places and prayed" (Luke 5:16). Amen.

36. RENEWAL

"The wind blows wherever it pleases. You hear its sound, but you cannot tell where it comes from or where it is going. So it is with everyone born of the Spirit" (John 3:8).

"But when the kindness and love of God appeared, he saved us, not because of righteous things we had done, but because of his mercy. He saved us through the washing of rebirth and renewal by the Holy Spirit, whom he poured out on us generously through Jesus Christ our Savior" (Titus 3:4-6).

"Restore us again, O God our Savior, and put away your displeasure toward us. . . . Will you not revive us again, that your people may rejoice in you?" (Psalm 85:4, 6).

Lord God,

On clear spring days I open the windows of my home and car to let the fresh air in. I need some fresh air in my soul, too.

Let the wind blow, Lord. Blow away the stale, stagnant stench of sin. Clean out the self-centeredness I should have discarded long ago. Prevent me from conforming to the ways of a world made rotten by rebellion against you.

Freshen up your church with a new sense of purpose, and use me to be a force for renewal in the body of Christ.

Renew my calling and my mission.

Wipe away the layers of dust that linger from sad memories and personal hurts.

Let a fresh wind blow in my family and among my friends. Refresh us all with your Spirit's power.

In the name of Christ and for his glory, make me a pure, clean vessel for your use. Renew me, Lord, with a keen sense of my calling and my mission. Let me be a breath of fresh air to all I encounter this week. Amen.

37. RESPECT

"Show proper respect to everyone: Love the brotherhood of believers, fear God, honor the king" (1 Peter 2:17).

Father in Heaven,

I live in a disrespectful culture. Angry, cynical, sarcastic remarks are the norm, and scorn for authority is commonplace. By contrast, you have called me to be respectful, showing honor to others out of reverence for Christ.

This week, help me to show proper respect to my coworkers by keeping my promises, by showing up on time for meetings, by picking up litter instead of expecting someone else to do it, by resolving conflicts through honest and respectful dialogue, by deferring to others instead of insisting on my own way, and by speaking about others with the loving-kindness that befits a follower of Jesus.

The Bible says to "love the brotherhood of believers," so Father, help me always to show proper respect for the church. While I recognize its flaws and weaknesses, may I always hold the church in high esteem because it is the body and bride of Christ, the household of God, the

Help me to show proper respect toward those to whom I am accountable at work.

assembly of the saved who have been bought with the precious blood of the Lamb. Let me never take for granted the privilege of being part of your church.

The Bible also reminds me to "honor the king," so help me to show proper respect for the governing authorities. Instead of simply finding fault with them, Lord, I pray for those who lead our nation and the other nations of the world. I pray for the President, for those who serve in Congress, for governors, mayors, and other local leaders. Give them direction and discernment so they will lead wisely and well. Remind me to be a faithful citizen who obeys the law and loves my neighbors.

Help me to show proper respect toward those to whom I am accountable at work. Teach me to live an honorable life, demonstrating integrity so that I myself will be worthy of others' respect.

Father, the Bible reminds me to "fear God" and respect you most of all. I hold you in the highest place of reverence. May my respect for you be reflected in the way I conduct myself this week. This is my prayer in the name of Christ. Amen. ☕

38. REST

"He makes me lie down in green pastures,
he leads me beside quiet waters" (Psalm 23:2).

"Come to me, all you who are weary and burdened,
and I will give you rest" (Matthew 11:28).

Father in Heaven,

Make me lie down.

I tend to keep moving. I live in such a fast-paced world that I'm always on the go. Make me slow down so I can hear your voice above the clatter and stress.

Father, you have provided green pastures where I can rest and quiet waters for me to enjoy. Forgive me when I get so busy and

Lead me to the quiet, peaceful waters.

distracted that I ignore them in favor of the deserts and dust of my familiar routines.

Help me not to let the days and weeks slip away without experiencing the times of refreshment my mind and body need. Lord, even more than a vacation or a day off, I need spiritual refreshment. Lead me to the quiet, peaceful waters where my soul will be renewed.

I pray in the name of the Lord of the Sabbath. Amen.

39. REVERENCE

"Come, let us bow down in worship, let us kneel before the Lord our Maker; for he is our God and we are the people of his pasture, the flock under his care"
(Psalm 95:6, 7).

"Our Father in heaven, hallowed be your name" (Matthew 6:9).

What a privilege it is to call you "Father"!

Because you are my Father, I know:
> You will always love me.
> You will always provide for me.
> You will discipline me for my good.
> You always want the best for me.

Because you are "*our* Father," I am not alone. You call me into relationship with others who are your children, my brothers and sisters, co-heirs in your glorious family.

Because you are holy:
> I will honor you as my Creator, my Leader, and my Lord.
> I will "hallow" your name. I will hold your name in awe
> and reverence and be careful not to misuse it.

I will hold your name in awe.

> I will worship you with my words and with my deeds.
> I will consider it a privilege to be called a Christian
> and to wear the name of Christ.

This week, may I hold your holy name in honor and reverence. Through Christ I pray. Amen.

40. SALVATION

"For God so loved the world that he gave his one and only Son, that whoever believes in him shall not perish but have eternal life" (John 3:16).

Dear God,

Thank you for the simplicity of the gospel and for its depth and power. Thank you for doing for me what I could never do for myself.

"*For God.*" You are the Creator of the universe, but you also are the Savior of my soul.

"*So loved.*" You love me with a love that is unselfish, generous, sacrificial and unending.

"*That he gave his one and only Son*"—the most expensive gift imaginable. Thank you for the painful and perfect sacrifice of Jesus, the sinless one who paid the price for my sins.

"*That whoever.*" Thank you for the breadth of your concern. You made your gift of grace freely available for all, so that whoever

> *Instead of dreading death*
> *I can look forward to heaven.*

wants to receive it may do so, no matter where they live or what they have done wrong.

"*Believes in him.*" You ask me for a personal response—to rely on your grace and obey your Word, not because I have all the answers, but because I trust you.

"*Shall not perish but have eternal life.*" You have given me a living hope, so instead of dreading death I can look forward to heaven. By your grace, in baptism I have been buried and raised up to new and everlasting life (Romans 6:1-4).

Father, help me never to lose my grip on the basics of the gospel. Let me never lose the wonder of it all. Let me never get so busy with my day-to-day work that I forget the price you paid to pave the way to heaven for me. I pray in the powerful name of your Son Jesus, whose very name means "the Lord saves" (Matthew 1:21). Amen. ☕

41. SERVICE

". . . Whoever wants to become great among you must be your servant, and whoever wants to be first must be your slave—just as the Son of Man did not come to be served, but to serve, and to give his life as a ransom for many" (Matthew 20:26, 27).

Father in Heaven,

I am your servant.
It's not my job to give the orders but to follow yours.
It's not my right to demand blessings from your hand but to humbly receive what you freely give.

I don't always know what is best; you always do.

Lord God, help me to see others the way you see them—as objects of your love. Assist me to serve others as Jesus did—

Help me to put others' needs ahead of my own.

down on his knees to wash dirty feet, reaching out with kind hands to touch the sick, going the extra mile to guide those who looked to him for leadership.

As a servant, I don't expect everything to go my way, but I trust you to work all things together for good. I don't expect everything to be easy, but I know that serving you will always be worthwhile.

This week, help me to put others' needs ahead of my own.

I want to give you my full obedience,
      My complete trust,
      And my highest honor.
For after all . . .
I am your servant.

I pray in the name of Jesus, who "made himself nothing, taking the very nature of a servant" (Philippians 2:7). Amen.

42. SPEECH

". . . The tongue is a small part of the body, but it makes great boasts. Consider what a great forest is set on fire by a small spark. The tongue also is a fire, a world of evil among the parts of the body. . . . Out of the same mouth come praise and cursing. My brothers, this should not be" (James 3:5, 6, 10).

Lord, help me to control my tongue.

In a vulgar world where profanity has become the norm, make my speech pure.

In a cruel world where it's common to tear others down, let my words build people up.

In a careless world where it's easy to say the wrong thing at the wrong time, help me to remember, "A man of knowledge uses words with restraint, and a man of understanding is even-tempered" (Proverbs 17:27).

Fill my workplace with healthy patterns of communication.

In a deceptive world where lies and manipulation are commonplace, let me be transparent and truthful in all things big and small.

In a cowardly world where it's easier to talk behind someone's back than to be honest and straightforward, help me to speak the truth in love.

In a prideful world where it's tempting to boast and engage in self-promotion to boost my own reputation, help me to speak words that are "helpful for building others up according to their needs" so that I can "benefit those who listen" (Ephesians 4:29).

In a world where corporate and political leaders often lack integrity, fill my workplace with healthy patterns of communication. Stop me from participating in any gossip or backbiting.

Help me to control my tongue. "There is . . . a time to be silent and a time to speak" (Ecclesiastes 3:7). Father, this week give me the wisdom to know when it's time to be silent, and the courage to say what needs to be said when it's time to speak up. This is my prayer in the name of Jesus, who said exactly what needed to be said—and also knew when to keep quiet. Amen. ☕

43. STEADFASTNESS

"Therefore, my dear brothers, stand firm. Let nothing move you. Always give yourselves fully to the work of the Lord, because you know that your labor in the Lord is not in vain" (1 Corinthians 15:58).

Father in Heaven,

Make me steady and strong in my faith. *Help me to stand firm on your Word*—believing it, teaching it, and putting it into practice.

Make me steady and strong in my work. Lord, you deserve my best effort. *I want to give myself fully to your work*—striving for

> *Help me to stand firmly on the bedrock principles of your Word.*

excellence, persevering till the job is done, working to make your church and my workplace the best they can be.

Make me steady and strong in hope. Remind me that *my labor in the Lord is never in vain*. Even one life changed for eternity makes all the effort worthwhile.

Help me to distinguish between your unchanging truth and human opinions that come and go. Help me to stand firmly on the bedrock principles of your Word but be flexible and pliable enough to respond to your Spirit's leading.

On Christ the solid rock I stand, and in his reliable and powerful name I pray. Amen. ☕

44. STEWARDSHIP

"Yours, O Lord, is the greatness and the power and the glory and the majesty and the splendor, for everything in heaven and earth is yours. Yours, O Lord, is the kingdom; you are exalted as head over all" (1 Chronicles 29:11).

"The earth is the Lord's, and everything in it, the world, and all who live in it" (Psalm 24:1).

It's all yours, Father.

This job.
This office.
This house.
This calendar and checkbook.

They're all yours, Father.
These coworkers.
These buildings and computers.
Every dollar received and spent.
Every minute that passes by.
Every life I touch.
Every person with whom I interact.

All of it belongs to you.

All of it belongs to you, Father.
My family and friends.
My customers, students, and neighbors.
My body and mind.
My talents and abilities.
My career.
My past, present, and future.

This week, help me to take good care of all these things. They belong to you.

I pray in the name of Christ, who said that to follow him we must give up everything we have (Luke 14:33). Amen.

45. SUBMISSION

"Your kingdom come, your will be done on earth as it is in heaven"
(Matthew 6:10).

Father,

Fill my heart with a deep concern for your kingdom. While I must focus on my day-to-day responsibilities, help me also to see the big picture. Remove from my heart any petty rivalries or short-sightedness that would cause me to care only about my own job or family or church or nation.

Give me a kingdom perspective so that I will rejoice in the victories achieved by your people wherever they are—on

I submit myself to your guidance and direction.

mission fields, in other countries, and in churches other than my own. I pray that people all over the world will acknowledge your sovereignty and receive your gift of salvation. May your kingdom come to the hearts of men and women everywhere.

I submit myself to your guidance and direction—my will surrendered to your will. In the words of David Livingstone, "Lord, send me anywhere, only go with me. Lay any burden on me, only sustain me. Sever any ties but the tie that binds me to Thy service and to Thy heart."

May your will be done. This week, guide me, Lord, to put your desires ahead of my own. In Christ I pray. Amen. ☕

46. TEMPTATION (I)

"And lead us not into temptation, but deliver us from the evil one"
(Matthew 6:13).

Dear Lord,

Temptation is part of my daily experience. I am tempted:

- To doubt when I should believe.
- To speak when I should listen.
- To be weak when I should be courageous.
- To be arrogant when I should be humble.
- To be self-centered when I should be concerned about others.
- To be silent when I should speak up.

Help me to "abstain from sinful desires,"
which war against my soul (1 Peter 2:11).

- To be coarse and vulgar when you have called me to be pure.
- To be greedy when you want me to be generous.
- To be harsh when you have called me to be kind.
- To complain when I should be thankful.
- To quit when I should keep going.

During the week ahead, help me to "abstain from sinful desires," which war against my soul (1 Peter 2:11). In times of temptation keep my priorities clear, and give me strength to resist what is wrong and do what is right.

I offer this prayer in the name of your Son, "who has been tempted in every way, just as we are—yet was without sin" (Hebrews 4:15). Amen. ☕

47. TEMPTATION (II)

"No temptation has seized you except what is common to man. And God is faithful; he will not let you be tempted beyond what you can bear. But when you are tempted, he will also provide a way out so that you can stand up under it" (1 Corinthians 10:13).

God of Goodness, Power and Might,

Protect me from the schemes of the adversary, the devil, who prowls about like a roaring lion, seeking whom he may devour. Protect me from moral failure. Protect my children as they face spiritual battles of their own. Steer my family and friends away from any attitudes or actions that would dishonor you or hinder our witness for the truth.

In these days of moral compromise, make us strong. In these days of doctrinal confusion, make our message clear. In these days of broken relationships, keep us together. In these days of sexual immorality, make our hearts pure. In these days of hypocrisy and duplicity, keep us honest. In these days of shallow commitment, draw our hearts toward you.

In these days when rebellion is common and cynicism prevails, teach us to be humble, faithful, gentle, respectful, and pure. In these days when life is cheap and justice is rare, help us to

Protect me from moral failure.

protect the innocent and stand up for the unborn, the aging, the disabled, and the weak. In these days when your Word is mocked and irreverence is common, make us holy people who honor and obey your revealed will from the heart.

Stay near to us. Keep Satan away from us. Deliver us from evil, O Lord. This is our prayer in the name of your Son Jesus, who told the tempter, "Away from me, Satan! For it is written: 'Worship the Lord your God, and serve him only'" (Matthew 4:10). Amen. ☕

48. TIME MANAGEMENT

"Teach us to number our days aright, that we may gain a heart of wisdom" (Psalm 90:12).

Everlasting Father,

You are eternal and timeless, the God of forever. Yet, time is one of your most precious gifts. I want to manage my time well, but it's difficult to do so in this hectic, frantic world. Since time management is an act of stewardship, Lord, I ask for your help.

Help me, Father . . .
• To plan my days wisely and to do so with humility, remembering that you can change my plans whenever you want.
• To organize my time well and keep your priorities foremost in my planning, so that my schedule will reflect what you consider most important.
• To put in an honest day's work, serving wholeheartedly and with a proper attitude, "as working for the Lord, not for men" (Colossians 3:23).

Time is one of your most precious gifts.

And Father, help me . . .
• To balance work with time for my family and friends, time for recreation, and time for spiritual renewal.
• To avoid wasting time. Weed out of my life any foolish and time-consuming pursuits that benefit no one.
• To accept occasional interruptions as opportunities for serving others. Help me to make the most of every opportunity—even the unexpected ones. Remind me that people are more important than any paper on my desk or any item on my to-do list. Help me to love and listen, to genuinely connect and care.

And Father, help me . . .
• To find adequate time for rest.
• To learn the secret of when to act decisively and when to wait patiently.
• To see life from your eternal perspective.

You are Lord of all my moments, all my days. Teach me to "number my days aright." I devote this day and this coming week to you in Jesus' name. Amen. ☕

49. UNITY

". . . That all of them may be one, Father, just as you are in me and I am in you. . . . May they be brought to complete unity to let the world know that you sent me" (John 17:21, 23).

"All the believers were one in heart and mind" (Acts 4:32).

Father,

Jesus prayed that his disciples would be united, so I pray for unity as well.

Show me how to preserve the unity of the Spirit through the bond of peace. Remind me that there is one body, one Spirit, one hope, one Lord, one faith, one baptism, one God and Father over all (Ephesians 4:4-6).

Forgive the uncharitable divisions that have become so widespread in your church. Pardon your followers for being so quick to attack our brothers and sisters and so slow to listen and to understand.

Give all of your people wisdom and patience as we relate to the body of Christ at large. Remind us that "we are not the only Christians, but we are Christians only."

> There is one body, one Spirit, one hope, one Lord, one faith, one baptism, one God and Father over all (Ephesians 4:4-6).

Forgive us for being so suspicious, so lacking in trust, so ready to pounce on those who disagree with us. Forgive us for choosing the quick road to division instead of the long and difficult path of reconciliation.

Teach us when to speak and when to remain silent, when to compromise and when to stand firm. Help us to discern the difference between clear biblical doctrines and our own personal opinions, traditions, and preferences. Even as we stand firm on your unchanging truth, keep us flexible and creative as we apply it to a changing world.

Make us one, Father. Unite us in the love and truth of Jesus Christ, who prayed for our unity on the night before he went to the cross. Amen. ☕

50. UNSELFISHNESS

"Not to us, O Lord, not to us but to your name be glory, because of your love and faithfulness" (Psalm 115:1).

It's not about me, Lord.

It's not about my comfort or convenience.
It's not about my preferences or pleasures.
It's not about my desires, my reputation, or my career.

This is your work.
It's your cause, your money, your church.
It's your mission and your will I'm here to fulfill.

These are your people you've given me to serve.
It's a privilege to invest in the lives that will providentially intersect with mine this week.

You are the Boss.

Help me to remember every moment, Lord,
That you are the Master.
You are the Boss.

It's not about me.
It's about you.

In Christ I pray. Amen. ☕

51. WISDOM

"If any of you lacks wisdom, he should ask God, who gives generously to all without finding fault, and it will be given to him" (James 1:5).

"Who is wise and understanding among you? Let him show it by his good life, by deeds done in the humility that comes from wisdom. . . . But the wisdom that comes from heaven is first of all pure; then peace loving, considerate, submissive, full of mercy and good fruit, impartial and sincere. Peacemakers who sow in peace raise a harvest of righteousness" (James 3:13, 17, 18).

This week, please give me wisdom, Father!

Fill me with godly common sense.
Anchor my thoughts in Scriptural truth.

Help me to handle money wisely and make financial decisions that reflect good stewardship of the resources you provide.

Strengthen my resolve, so that I will make wise choices guided by the moral compass of your Word.

Enable me to make decisions that will benefit those who work with me and those I serve.

Wisdom "is more profitable than silver and yields better returns than gold" (Proverbs 3:14).

Show me how to handle the challenges of living for Christ in a complex world that's adrift in moral relativism.

I agree with Solomon, who wrote that wisdom "is more profitable than silver and yields better returns than gold" (Proverbs 3:14).

Give me wisdom, Lord. This is my prayer in the name of your wise and holy Son, Jesus Christ, "in whom are hidden all the treasures of wisdom and knowledge" (Colossians 2:3). Amen.

52. WORRY

"Therefore, I tell you, do not worry about your life, what you will eat or drink; or about your body, what you will wear. Is not life more important than food, and the body more important than clothes? Look at the birds of the air; they do not sow or reap or store away in barns, and yet your heavenly Father feeds them. Are you not much more valuable than they? Who of you by worrying can add a single hour to his life? . . . Therefore do not worry about tomorrow, for tomorrow will worry about itself. Each day has enough trouble of its own" (Matthew 6:25-27, 34).

"Give me a good digestion, Lord,
And also something to digest.
Give me a healthy body, Lord,
With sense to keep it at its best.

Give me a healthy mind, O Lord,
To keep the good and pure in sight,
Which seeing wrong is not appalled
But finds a way to put it right.

Give me a mind that is not bored,
That does not whimper, whine or sigh.
Don't let me worry over-much
About that fussy thing called 'I.'

Give me a sense of humor, Lord.
Give me the grace to see a joke,
To get some happiness from life
And pass it on to other folk. Amen."

—An adaptation of an ancient monk's prayer from
Glastonbury Abbey, England (author unknown)

Lord God,

How often I have violated the plain teachings of Jesus!

Jesus said not to worry about what I eat and drink, but I arrange my schedule around mealtimes and concern myself with food far more than I should. Jesus said not to worry about clothes, but my culture places fashion ahead of faith and puts more emphasis on keeping up appearances than on keeping your commandments.

You feed the birds and clothe the lilies, so I can trust you to feed and clothe me. Forgive me for worrying about such things.

And forgive me for worrying about other things: my job, my health, my money, my family, and my future. Help me to distinguish between legitimate concern and sinful worry; to accept the responsibilities of leadership without being

I will lift up every concern to you.

overcome by them; to care for my loved ones without taking on burdens you never intended for me to bear alone. I can't control the weather, the stock market, or the attitudes and actions of everyone around me, but I can trust you in all circumstances.

So this week, I choose not to be consumed by anxiety, but instead I will lift up every concern to you and place it in your strong hands. Father, I offer this prayer in the name of Jesus, who promised that you "give good gifts to those who ask" (Matthew 7:11). Amen.

PRAYERS FOR SPECIAL DAYS AND SEASONS

NEW YEAR'S DAY (I)

"Forget the former things; do not dwell on the past. See, I am doing a new thing! Now it springs up; do you not perceive it?" (Isaiah 43:18, 19).

"Therefore, if anyone is in Christ, he is a new creation; the old has gone, the new has come!" (2 Corinthians 5:17).

"He who was seated on the throne said, 'I am making everything new!'" (Revelation 21:5).

Lord God, Creator of Heaven and Earth,

You are the author of new beginnings! You spoke the universe into existence and created all things new at the beginning of time. Now as another year begins, please:

- Give me a fresh perspective so I can see the opportunities you are placing before me in the new year.
- Renew my strength to face every challenge the coming months will bring.
- Allow me to learn new things about you and influence more people in the right direction.

Show me new ways of doing things.

- Help me to grow. Give me new ideas, show me new ways of doing things, and grant me new insights I can share with others.
- Renew my sense of purpose, and fill me with fresh energy for each day's tasks.

In the name of Jesus I dedicate this new day and this new year to you. Amen.

NEW YEAR'S DAY (II)

"Forgetting what is behind and straining toward what is ahead, I press on toward the goal to win the prize for which God has called me heavenward in Christ Jesus" (Philippians 3:13, 14).

Father,

As the morning sun marks a fresh beginning to this new day, we offer you praise and thanksgiving. We offer and devote body and soul, all that we are and all that we have, to your service and glory.

This year, let us receive every day as a gift from you—as if it were a resurrection from death to a new enjoyment of life.

Every day is a gift from you.

Enable us to meet every rising sun with appreciation for your goodness, as if you had created each day new just for us.

Our hearts praise and magnify you, our good and glorious Creator. May you be pleased with all we do on this new day and in this new year. Through Christ we pray. Amen. ☕

—Paraphrased from *A Serious Call to a Devout and Holy Life* (1728), by William Law

PRESIDENT'S DAY

"The king's heart is in the hand of the Lord" (Proverbs 21:1).

*The following excerpts are quoted from the inaugural addresses
of those who have served as President of the United States.*

. . . I shall take my present leave; but not without resorting
once more to the benign Parent of the Human Race in
humble supplication that, since He has been pleased to
favor the American people with opportunities for deliberating
in perfect tranquility . . . so His divine blessing may be
equally conspicuous in the enlarged views, the temperate
consultations, and the wise measures on which the success of
this Government must depend. (George Washington, 1789)

And may that Being who is supreme over all, the Patron of
Order, the Fountain of Justice, and the Protector in all ages of
the world of virtuous liberty, continue His blessing upon this
nation and its Government and give it all possible success and
duration consistent with the ends of His providence.
(John Adams, 1797)

. . . Knowing that "except the Lord keep the city the watchman
waketh but in vain," with fervent supplications for His favor, to

*Let us invoke His aid and His
blessings upon our labors.*

His overruling providence I commit with humble but fearless
confidence my own fate and the future destinies of my country.
(John Quincy Adams, 1825)

With malice toward none, with charity for all, with firmness in the
right as God gives us to see the right, let us strive on to finish
the work we are in, to bind up the nation's wounds, to care for
him who shall have borne the battle and for his widow and his
orphan, to do all which may achieve and cherish a just and
lasting peace among ourselves and with all nations.
(Abraham Lincoln, 1865)

And let us not trust to human effort alone, but humbly
acknowledging the power and goodness of Almighty God, who
presides over the destiny of nations, and who has at all times
been revealed in our country's history, let us invoke His aid and
His blessings upon our labors. (Grover Cleveland, 1885) ➤

My fellow-citizens, no people on earth have more cause to be thankful than ours, and this is said reverently, in no spirit of boastfulness in our own strength, but with gratitude to the Giver of Good who has blessed us with the conditions which have enabled us to achieve so large a measure of well-being and of happiness. (Theodore Roosevelt, 1905)

In this dedication of a Nation we humbly ask the blessing of God. May He protect each and every one of us. May He guide me in the days to come. (Franklin D. Roosevelt, 1933)

. . . Let us go forth to lead the land we love, asking His blessing and His help, but knowing that here on earth God's work must truly be our own. (John F. Kennedy, 1961)

Now we hear again the echoes of our past: a general falls to his knees in the hard snow of Valley Forge; a lonely President paces the darkened halls, and ponders his struggle to preserve the Union; the men of the Alamo call out encouragement to

We raise our voices to the God who is the Author of this most tender music.

each other; a settler pushes west and sings a song, and the song echoes out forever and fills the unknowing air. It is the American sound. It is hopeful, big-hearted, idealistic, daring, decent, and fair. That's our heritage; that is our song. We sing it still. For all our problems, our differences, we are together as of old, as we raise our voices to the God who is the Author of this most tender music. And may He continue to hold us close as we fill the world with our sound—sound in unity, affection, and love—one people under God, dedicated to the dream of freedom that He has placed in the human heart, called upon now to pass that dream on to a waiting and hopeful world. (Ronald Reagan, 1985)

We go forward with complete confidence in the eventual triumph of freedom. Not because history runs on the wheels of inevitability; it is human choices that move events. Not because we consider ourselves a chosen nation; God moves and chooses as He wills. We have confidence because freedom is the permanent hope of mankind, the hunger in dark places, the longing of the soul. When our Founders declared a new order of the ages; when soldiers died in wave upon wave for a union based on liberty; when citizens marched in peaceful outrage under the banner "Freedom Now"—they were acting on an ancient hope that is meant to be fulfilled. History has an ebb and flow of justice, but history also has a visible direction, set by liberty and the Author of Liberty. (George W. Bush, 2005)

With hope and virtue, let us brave once more the icy currents, and endure what storms may come. Let it be said by our children's children that when we were tested we refused to let this journey end, that we did not turn back, nor did we falter; and with eyes fixed on the horizon and God's grace upon us, we carried forth that great gift of freedom and delivered it safely to future generations. (Barack Obama, 2009)

Note: The above quotes are from complete transcripts of Presidential Inaugural Addresses available through Yale Law School's Lillian Goldman Law Library at http://avalon.law.yale.edu.

GOOD FRIDAY AND EASTER (I)

"From that time on Jesus began to explain to his disciples that he must go to Jerusalem and suffer many things at the hands of the elders, chief priests and teachers of the law, and that he must be killed and on the third day be raised to life" (Matthew 16:21).

Heavenly Father,

During this holy week keep me focused on **the path your Son walked**. It was a path that brought him from heaven to earth as "the Word became flesh and dwelt among us." It was a path that caused him to wrestle with the same temptations and stresses I face—but his path led to the Garden of Gethsemane and the cross of Calvary.

Help me to understand **the plan your Son fulfilled**. It was a plan you had in mind long before I was born—a plan foretold by the Old Testament prophets and further revealed by the New Testament apostles. It was a plan to restore my hope, forgive my sin, and bring me back into fellowship with you and with others.

As I approach Good Friday, help me to keep in mind **the pain your Son endured**. The physical pain of crucifixion—nails pounded through his hands and feet, the scourging of his back, the crown of thorns upon his head. The emotional pain

The cross is not the end of the story.

of rejection and betrayal, loneliness and abandonment. The spiritual pain of bearing the weight of the world's sins and paying the price for sinners' disobedience, even though as a flawless Passover Lamb he never committed a sin himself. May I always be filled with gratitude and wonder as I contemplate his sacrifice.

Most of all, help me to remember **the purpose your Son achieved**. Thank you, Father, that the cross is not the end of the story. Thank you for the empty tomb, the good news of Easter, and the life-changing reality of grace.

You are the author of new life. This is a holy week, but because of your Son, every week and every day are holy times. Help me, Father, to remember that:

- Jesus' resurrection is a fact, not only on the brightest morning but also during the darkest night.
- Resurrection hope isn't a once-a-year holiday; it's an everyday reality.

Let me live every day in the afterglow of the resurrection. Prepare me to "give an answer to anyone who asks the reason for the hope that I have" (1 Peter 3:15). I pray in the name of our risen Lord. Amen. ☕

GOOD FRIDAY AND EASTER (II)

"Later, Joseph of Arimathea asked Pilate for the body of Jesus. Now Joseph was a disciple of Jesus, but secretly because he feared the Jews. With Pilate's permission, he came and took the body. He was accompanied by Nicodemus, the man who earlier had visited Jesus at night. Nicodemus brought a mixture of myrrh and aloes, about seventy-five pounds. Taking Jesus' body, the two of them wrapped it, with the spices, in strips of linen. This was in accordance with Jewish burial customs. At the place where Jesus was crucified, there was a garden, and in the garden a new tomb, in which no one had ever been laid. Because it was the Jewish day of Preparation and since the tomb was nearby, they laid Jesus there" (John 19:38-42).

Father,

How humble and simple was the funeral of Jesus!

Two men took his body down from the cross, wrapped it in linen cloth, and placed it in a tomb cut out of rock. A small group of women watched, and a couple of days later they came bearing spices to anoint the body.

That was all.

Even his closest friends weren't there for the burial. They were huddled behind closed doors, confused and afraid.

His name and his fame endure.

No cheering throng showed up. No kings and dignitaries. No TV reporters and media coverage . . . just some Gospel writers with papyri and pens.

Yet how glorious was the aftermath! Within days, hundreds witnessed the reality of his resurrection. Within weeks, thousands were baptized in his name. Within years, millions accepted him. Centuries later, his name and his fame endure and surpass all other accomplishments of men.

Father, help me to keep my eyes on your Son Jesus. Let me serve in the power of the risen Lord, whose glorious name towers above all others. Amen. ☕

GOOD FRIDAY AND EASTER (III)

"For what I received I passed on to you as of first importance: that Christ died for our sins according to the Scriptures, that he was buried, that he was raised on the third day according to the Scriptures" (1 Corinthians 15:3, 4).

Father,

Help me to remember what is "of first importance."

Other matters that the world considers important fade in comparison to the death, burial, and resurrection of Christ. My worries and cares seem trivial when I view them in the light of eternity. My daily labors, the problems I must solve, the rigors

> *Help me to live every day in the shadow of the cross and the triumph of the empty tomb.*

of personal relationships, the weariness of making a living—somehow they all seem more manageable when I remember that you have the ability to raise the dead!

Lord God, prevent me from turning my Palm Sunday, Good Friday, and Easter traditions into little more than springtime holidays. Help me to live every day in the shadow of the cross and the triumph of the empty tomb.

Fix my mind on what you consider most important. Show me how to "keep the main thing the main thing." Keep me focused on the heart of the gospel, not on the peripheral issues that disturb and divide.

Bless me this week, Father, as I draw near to you through the crucified and risen Christ. Amen. ☕

MOTHER'S DAY

"May your father and mother be glad; may she who gave you birth rejoice!"
(Proverbs 23:25).

"Her children arise and call her blessed; her husband also, and he praises her:
'Many women do noble things, but you surpass them all.' Charm is deceptive,
and beauty is fleeting; but a woman who fears the Lord is to be praised"
(Proverbs 31:28-30).

"I have been reminded of your sincere faith, which first lived in your
grandmother Lois and in your mother Eunice and, I am persuaded,
now lives in you also" (2 Timothy 1:5).

Dear God,

Thank you for our mothers.

They are nurses, counselors, philosophers, cooks, listeners, coaches, problem-solvers, theologians, hug-givers and hurt-soothers. They are some of the most influential instructors we'll ever encounter.

Moses' mother relied on you in uncertain times. Samuel's mother dedicated her son to your service. Jesus' mother demonstrated strong faith. Timothy's mom taught him the Scriptures. Our mothers have taught us important lessons, too.

Thank you for the women in our lives who deserve the respect of a grateful family and nation.

They serve on the front lines of our culture. Their values shape our worldview. Their love provides a safe harbor in an ocean of insecurity. When we were hungry, they fed us. When we were sick, they sat at our bedside.

Even now, when we are tempted to stray from your path, their love is a magnet to pull us back. Thank you for their faithfulness!

And Lord, on this Mother's Day we pray for the widows who have no one to send them a card or buy them flowers. We pray for the mothers of prodigal sons and daughters from whom no card or phone call will come. We pray for those who grieve because of the death of a child, or who cry because of their mother's illness or death. We pray for single moms who struggle to keep their heads above water; for birth moms who made the courageous choice to place their babies in adoptive homes; and for women who would like to be mothers, but they have remained unmarried and childless or have faced the frustration of infertility.

Lord, on this Mother's Day we thank you for the women in our lives who deserve the respect of a grateful family and nation. Bless them and surround them with your love on this special day. This is our prayer in the name of Jesus, who cared for his mother even when he was dying on the cross. Amen.

GRADUATION

. . . .

"May the grace of the Lord Jesus Christ, and the love of God, and the fellowship of the Holy Spirit be with you all" (2 Corinthians 13:14).

The following blessing is often spoken during commencement ceremonies at Cincinnati Christian University.

So you will know which way to go in the future, may you never forget how God has led you in the past.

So you will know how to lead others, may you first be a true follower of Jesus Christ.

So you will never be alone, may you always remember that God is with you.

So you will be strong, may you always rely on the Lord for your strength.

So you will earn the right to be heard, may you always be a man or woman of integrity—a person worth listening to.

So you will be powerful in your influence, may you first be humble and gentle, with a servant's heart.

Always remember that God is with you.

So you will know God ever more deeply, may you always hunger and thirst for righteousness.

So you will know the joy that comes from serving over the long haul, may you persevere and remain faithful even when hardship comes.

So you will continue discovering and doing God's will, may the Lord grant you a teachable mind and an unceasing devotion to prayer.

So you will remember your purpose in life, may you have an unquenchable passion for ministry and the determination to complete the work God has given you to do.

So you will be sympathetic toward those who suffer, may you always have a tender heart for those who are lost without Christ and for those live under the burden of injustice.

May you always be true to your word, strong in your faith, abounding in love.

And most of all, in the name of Christ, may "The Lord bless you and keep you; the Lord make his face shine upon you and be gracious to you; the Lord turn his face toward you, and give you peace" (Numbers 6:24-26). Amen.

FATHER'S DAY

"As a father has compassion on his children, so the Lord has compassion on those who fear him" (Psalm 103:13).

"Because you are sons, God sent the Spirit of his Son into our hearts, the Spirit who calls out, 'Abba, Father'" (Galatians 4:6).

Father in Heaven,

I'm so glad I can call you that: "Abba, Father."

"How great is the love the Father has lavished on us, that we should be called children of God! And that is what we are!" (1 John 3:1).

Thank you for giving us what we all long to receive from our dads. You provide for us and protect us from harm. You listen and pay attention to us. You discipline, correct, and guide us. You set a flawless example for us to follow.

We pray for all of the men among us who are fathers. Give us wisdom, courage, and strength to lead our children well.

> *Give us wisdom, courage, and strength to lead our children well.*

We pray for all of us who miss our fathers because death, distance, or dysfunction has removed them from our lives. And we pray for all who feel frustrated and angry with our fathers. Show us how to honor them. Give us grace to forgive the imperfections of our earthly fathers, and to find in you the perfect Father we need.

Through Christ we pray. Amen.

FOURTH OF JULY (I)

"I urge then, first of all, that requests, prayers, intercession and thanksgiving be made for everyone—for kings and all those in authority, that we may live peaceful and quiet lives in all godliness and holiness" (1 Timothy 2:1, 2).

"We think it is incumbent upon this people to humble themselves before God on account of their sins. . . . [And] also to implore the Divine Blessing upon us, that by the assistance of His grace, we may be enabled to reform whatever is amiss among us, so God may be pleased to continue giving us the blessings we enjoy."
—John Hancock, the first signer of the Declaration of Independence

Lord God,

As the USA celebrates another birthday on the 4th of July, we recognize that you hold the whole world in your hands. As your Word instructs, we pray for the leaders of our nation and for those who lead all the nations on earth.

Guide those who serve as presidents, prime ministers, governors, senators, members of Congress and Parliament, mayors, and others in governmental authority.

Give them extraordinary wisdom as they wrestle with complicated issues. Give them the courage to stand for what is right, not merely what is popular or politically expedient.

Provide them with physical health, clarity of mind, and purity of heart. Protect them and their families from the unique spiritual and emotional dangers that surround those in roles of high visibility and authority.

Help them to put their calling above their careers, to submit their personal ambitions to your will and to the common good, and to be more concerned about their people than they are about their

You hold the whole world in your hands.

positions of power. Help them to understand and fulfill your purpose for government—to uphold justice and "to punish those who do wrong and to commend those who do right" (1 Peter 2:14).

➤

Show them how to be good stewards of the resources you have generously bestowed upon our world.

Thank you, Lord, for public servants in every nation who desire to serve you and serve their people. May we always encourage them in their noble work.

Help us to be faithful citizens of our nation, Lord, who vote according to Christian principles and set an example that makes the teaching of Christ attractive. Most of all, help us, Lord, to make disciples in all nations of the earth.

Bring your righteousness to the forefront, Lord, so that in every nation your people will be able to live "peaceful and quiet lives in all godliness and holiness." We pray in the name of the King of kings. Amen. ☕

FOURTH OF JULY (II)

The following prayer was written by Roy Mays III, a graduate of Cincinnati Christian University who served on the staff at Southland Christian Church in Lexington, Kentucky, prior to his death in 2005. Roy delivered this prayer in Washington, D. C., at the beginning of a session of the U.S. House of Representatives. It's published in the Congressional Record *of the 107th Congress, September 6, 2001. Reprinted by permission of the Mays family.*

Dear Gracious Father,

For years we have sung "America, America, God shed his grace on thee," and in this prayer we affirm you have done it, and we ask you to do it again.

As the giver of grace, we need your presence and assistance, your good favor and great power. For whatever situation we face today, show us that your strength is sufficient.

On the day following my diagnosis with myeloma cancer, you gave me an insight for experiencing grace in the metaphor of a railroad track. One rail represented healing, and one rail symbolized dealing. I was invited to embrace your grace and

> *For whatever situation we face today, show us that your strength is sufficient.*

endure my race, keeping both rails parallel or I would wreck. Your part was to establish your purpose and supply your power. My part was to pray and persevere.

For all of the Members of this House and those they represent, we implore you to please touch us with your healing grace. Forgive us when we have forgotten you. Lift us up when we have let you down. Deliver help to those who are hurting, and provide peace for those who are in pain.

Also, we entreat you to please give us your dealing grace: wisdom for our work, discernment for our decisions, resources for our responsibilities, and joy for our journey.

In all these requests, Heavenly Father, we pray that your will be done, and we accept that your grace is sufficient. For Thine is the kingdom and the power and the glory, forever and ever. Amen. ☙

TIMES OF REPENTANCE

"Restore us again, O God our Savior, and put away your displeasure toward us. . . . Will you not revive us again, that your people may rejoice in you? Show us your unfailing love, O Lord, and grant us your salvation" (Psalm 85:4-7).

Father,

Forgive us, for we know all too well what we're doing.

We know the good we ought to do and don't do it, and that's a sin (James 4:17).

We know we ought to pray without ceasing, but often we try to exist without praying.

We say that experience is the best teacher, but we try to avoid your spiritual classroom.

Renew our souls with a fresh taste of amazing grace.

We tell others that trials build character, but when trials come our way we quickly head for the nearest exit.

We know we shouldn't worry or hold grudges, yet our anxious thoughts cling like thistles, and old resentments irritate like pebbles in our shoes.

We know Jesus died to wipe the slate clean, but like stubborn streaks on a windowpane our past sins cloud our eyes and blur our vision.

We can quote the 23rd Psalm, but we've failed to shepherd our people. We've turned the Great Commission into a great omission. We're preoccupied with our great commitments to the golf game and the soap opera, the stock market and the health spa.

We know how quickly our kids are growing up, but we find so little time to read a book, fly a kite, tell a joke, toss a ball, or pass along a memory.

We've read the New Testament's "one another" passages, but it's hard to find time for one another when we're rushing from one meeting to another, one store to another, one job to another, one game to another.

We know we ought to exercise self-control, but it's hard in the days of remote control, cruise control, and a nation's moral climate that seems out of control. We know that our bodies are temples, yet we abuse them by overworking, overeating, under-resting, and under-exercising.

Forgive us, Father. We know exactly what we're doing.
We know that your Word is a lamp to our feet and a light to our path, but we're often too lazy to turn off the TV and open the Book.

We know that we thrive on encouragement ourselves, yet we're quick to criticize others. We know that friends are precious gifts, but we can't seem to find the time to simply sit and talk, write a note, or make a phone call to friends who need these gifts from us.

We know that the church is the beautiful bride of Christ, but often we treat her like a scorned woman. We're sloppy in our worship and sluggish in our service. We're fussy with our expectations, but we seldom ask about yours.

Sometimes we say, "If I'd only known . . . ." But we already know so much! Help us, Father, to "live up to what we have already attained" (Philippians 3:16). Help us to seek your kingdom first, to love our families well, to devote ourselves to prayer. Help us to find fellowship instead of finding fault. When temptation tugs, keep us faithful. When regrets threaten to overwhelm us, renew our souls with a fresh taste of amazing grace.

We pray in the name of Jesus, who died in our place and lives to give us life. Amen. ☕

TIMES OF TRAGEDY

In January 2010 an earthquake devastated the nation of Haiti. Soon afterward, the *Cincinnati Enquirer* published a provocative editorial cartoon. The left side of the cartoon showed the rubble of the earthquake along with a sign that said, "Act of God." The right side of the cartoon showed a drawing of Uncle Sam reaching out his hand along with a sign that said, "Act of Humanity." Clearly the Lord doesn't need anyone to defend his honor, but the cartoon provoked a response and helped to shape the prayer I wrote for that Monday morning.

"God is our refuge and strength, an ever-present help in trouble. Therefore we will not fear, though the earth give way and the mountains fall . . . and the mountains quake with their surging" (Psalm 46:1-3).

Dear God,

On behalf of the suffering crowds in Haiti, we cry out to you. Disturbing questions crowd our minds and sadness fills our hearts when we see the news reports. Our brothers and sisters in Haiti have already suffered so much, this earthquake seems an especially crushing blow.

Lord, why did you allow the earth to shake in this already-fragile land? Why didn't you step in when so many homes began to crumble? Why so many children dying, so many long-suffering souls pushed beyond reasonable limits of endurance? Why have you tolerated corrupt government leaders there who siphoned off

In spite of our questions, we choose to trust in your goodness, and we volunteer to be your instruments of blessing.

the country's wealth and enriched themselves at the expense of their people? Just as the prophets complained in Old Testament times, we can't help but cry out and say, "How long, O Lord, must we call for help?" Sometimes we wonder if you're really listening.

And yet . . . something deep within us knows you are not to be blamed for what's wrong with this broken and dying world. Despite the sorrow and pain, help us to see the "acts of God" in:

- The hardy perseverance of your people in Haiti who continue to trust in you;
- The compassionate and sacrificial response of the medical and military personnel who rushed to Haiti to assist the wounded and dying;
- The faithful service of the missionaries and other Christian leaders who dedicated their lives to the people of Haiti long before the current crisis, and who will stay there long after this crisis is over; and
- The generous gifts of all who swiftly sent financial support to aid those in need.

Let us see the "acts of God" in the churches that quickly stepped up to help, the families who stand ready to adopt homeless children, and the social service agencies that are doing what they can. Let us see your acts in the privileges and responsibilities you have given us to dwell in a nation where we're blessed with the means to assist those in desperate need.

Most of all, let us see the "acts of God" in the hopeful and comforting words of Scripture, which remind us that no matter how bad things get on this earth, you are here with us and you care. You do answer prayer, and often you use ordinary people like us as conduits of blessing. You are familiar with innocent suffering and gross injustice because it happened to you at the cross. You are the one who brings life out of death, renewal out of ruin, and victory out of misery.

So in spite of our questions, we choose to trust in your goodness, and we volunteer to be your instruments of blessing to serve and assist those in need in Haiti and elsewhere around the world. In the words of Martin Luther King, Jr., "Faith is taking the first step even when you don't see the whole staircase"—and we are willing to take that step. We are "convinced that neither death nor life, neither angels nor demons, neither the present nor the future, nor any powers, neither height nor depth, nor anything else in all creation, will be able to separate us from the love of God that is in Christ Jesus our Lord" (Romans 8:38, 39).

Even in the most difficult times, this blessed assurance is real. So we ask you to be a refuge and strength for your people in Haiti right now, Father. This is our prayer in the name of Christ. Amen. ☙

THANKSGIVING (I)

"Enter his gates with thanksgiving and his courts with praise; give thanks to him and praise his name. For the Lord is good and his love endures forever; his faithfulness continues through all generations" (Psalm 100:4, 5).

Gracious God,

Thank you for all you have done for us.

As our loving Father, you have provided our needs, answered our prayers, and protected our hearts.

As our God of mercy and grace, you have forgiven our sins and rescued us from the condemnation we deserve.

As the Lord over all nations, you have granted us freedom and responsibility to serve you and to take the gospel to the world. We are grateful for the partnership we share in your kingdom work.

We've seen your hand of blessing over and over again.

As the source of love and the architect of healthy relationships, you have enriched our lives through friends and loved ones who care about us and who share our joys and sorrows.

As the ever-present Lord of life, you have been with us in times of sickness and stress, through large and small victories, through the daily grind as well as through unusual moments of special grace. We've seen your hand of blessing over and over again.

Best of all, you have given us your Son Jesus Christ to be our Savior. In his name we simply say thank you, Father. You have been good to us, and we are grateful. Amen. ☕

THANKSGIVING (II)

"Let everything that has breath praise the Lord" (Psalm 150:6).

O God,

so beautiful are your ways.
>As autumn's splendor now unfolds,
>The hills ablaze with reds and golds,
>We glimpse the wealth your hand upholds:

Creation sings your praise.

O God, so personal are your ways.
>Like a shepherd with your sheep,
>Our names you know, our souls you keep,
>Protected even as we sleep:

Your people sing your praise.

O God, so merciful are your ways.
>You've swept away the curse of sin
>And made our lives begin again.
>Saved by grace, renewed within:

Forgiven, we sing your praise.

O God, so bountiful are your ways.
>Rich blessings we can see and hear,
>Food and shelter, loved ones dear,
>The joy of your own presence here:

Grateful, we sing your praise.

O God, so wonderful are your ways.
>Beyond the stars, Lord, you are there.
>Through all the world, you see, you care,
>And stoop to hear our humble prayer:

In awe, we sing your praise.

Amen.

THANKSGIVING (III)

"And whatever you do, whether in word or deed, do it all in the name of the Lord Jesus, giving thanks to God the Father through him" (Colossians 3:17).

"Give thanks in all circumstances, for this is God's will for you in Christ Jesus" (1 Thessalonians 5:18).

Father,

Before we count our blessings, help us first to notice them.

Thank you for the big things you have done for us:
>For loving us in spite of our rebellion,
>For filling us with hope through your Son's resurrection,
>For sustaining your church over the last two thousand years.

And thank you for the little things you have done for us:
>For days off and extra hours of sleep,
>For pumpkin pie and homemade bread,
>For soft beds, hot showers, and full refrigerators.

Thank you for the blessings we hold in our hands,
Like paychecks, Bibles, and grandchildren.

Thank you for the blessings we hardly even see.

And thank you for the blessings we hardly even see,
Like the quiet spiritual growth that's happening every day in us.

Thank you for the familiar blessings we celebrate every Thanksgiving, and for the ways you continually give us new challenges to face, new lessons to learn, and new blessings to enjoy.

Thank you for all you've done for us, Lord. In Jesus' name. Amen. ☕

CHRISTMAS (I)

"The people walking in darkness have seen a great light; on those living in the land of the shadow of death a light has dawned. . . . For to us a child is born, to us a son is given, and the government will be on his shoulders. And he will be called Wonderful Counselor, Mighty God, Everlasting Father, Prince of Peace" (Isaiah 9:2, 6).

Lord God,

I pray that this busy season of the year will mean more than just the fleeting fun of a holiday. Let it be a time of spiritual growth—a time to gain a greater appreciation for your grace.

When things seem dark, remind me to live in your light.
When my burdens seem heavy, help me remember that the government is on your shoulders, not on mine.

When I need comfort and advice, thank you for being the Wonderful Counselor who gives me solace and strength.
You are the Mighty God, so when I feel powerless, I will depend on you.

When things seem dark, remind me to live in your light.

When life passes by quickly and there never seems to be enough time to get everything done, you are the Everlasting Father. When conflicts abound, you are the Prince of Peace.

Father, your Son Jesus is more than just the reason for the season. He's the reason I can approach your throne of grace all year 'round. I pray in his holy name. Amen.

CHRISTMAS (II)

"But the angel said to them, 'Do not be afraid. I bring you good news of great joy that will be for all the people. Today in the town of David a Savior has been born to you; he is Christ the Lord'" (Luke 2:10, 11).

Father in Heaven,

Make us like Mary, who had the faith to accept a seemingly impossible task by saying simply, "I am the Lord's servant—may it be to me as you have said."

Make us like Joseph, who responded to a very difficult situation by courageously obeying your Word and faithfully serving his family.

Make us like the shepherds of Bethlehem, receptive to the message of the angels and willing to realize that no other task is more important than being in the presence of the Christ-child.

Make us like those faithful old saints Anna and Simeon, who recognized the fulfillment of your plans and saw in the face of an infant your long-awaited gift of grace.

Make us like the wise men, who traveled long distances seeking the young Messiah-King and presented him their best gifts.

Christmas isn't a religious myth or a childish fable.

Most of all, make us like Jesus, who humbled himself and took the form of a servant—making himself poor so we could receive the riches of heaven.

Lord God, thank you that Christmas isn't a religious myth or a childish fable. It isn't merely a secular holiday or an excuse for self-indulgence. It's a season to remember that you, the God of all eternity, loved us enough to intervene in history through your Son Jesus Christ. May every one of us keep Christ at the center of our hearts today and throughout the coming year. In his name we pray. Amen. ☕

"So Joseph also went up from the town of Nazareth in Galilee to Judea, to Bethlehem the town of David, because he belonged to the house and line of David. He went there to register with Mary, who was pledged to be married to him and was expecting a child. While they were there, the time came for the baby to be born, and she gave birth to her firstborn, a son. She wrapped him in cloths and placed him in a manger, because there was no room for them in the inn"
(Luke 2:4-7).

Father,

The approach of the Christmas season reminds us how much you value our families. When you sent your Son to earth, you placed him in a human family—born to Mary, nurtured by Joseph, sharing his home with younger brothers and sisters.

Thank you for our families, Father. We know that Satan would like nothing better than to destroy our homes, and we also know

Bless our families with peace and joy.

that the proving-ground for our own leadership begins among those who know us best.

Protect our marriages. Guide us to honor and respect those among us who are single. Help us to be effective and conscientious parents. Protect our children from evil influences that would harm them or move them away from you. Strengthen the bonds of fellowship among your people so that all can experience a sense of "family" within the church.

Though our families are imperfect, give us grace to forgive, and help us to make our relationships with our loved ones the best they can be. For those who are parents, grant us patience and understanding with our children and grandchildren. For those who are married, Lord, we pray that you will expand all our efforts to love, honor, and respect our partners and be faithful to them in all things.

During this busy Christmas season and throughout the coming year, bless our homes, Lord God. Bless our families with peace and joy.

We ask this in the name of Christ. Amen. ☕

NEW YEAR'S EVE

"It is finished"–Jesus (John 19:30).

Dear Lord,

I want to finish well.

Help me to conclude this year in a way that honors you.

In the new year ahead, give me new vigor and a renewed sense of purpose.

Help me to finish each day well so that I can go to bed at night in a peaceful relationship with you, with others, and with myself.

Help me to finish each season of service well. May each chapter of my life and my career find me faithful and fruitful.

Help me to finish each task well. Enable me to serve with excellence, giving my best effort on jobs I enjoy and ones I find

Let my faith never waver and my vision never dim.

tedious. Whether I'm doing the mundane or the magnificent, remind me that I am working for you, and you deserve my best.

Most of all, Lord, help me to finish my life well. Keep me true to my values, focused on my goals, and loyal to the people who rely on me. Let my faith never waver and my vision never dim.

When I come to the end of my days, may I be able to say with Jesus, "It is finished," knowing that my eternal joy in your presence has only just begun. I pray in the name of Christ, who is the Alpha and the Omega, the Beginning and the End. Amen. ☕

....

To order more copies of this book or others written by David Faust,
please visit the Cincinnati Christian University bookstore,
www.CCUniversity.edu/bookstore.

If you would like to receive a Monday Morning Prayer
every week via e-mail, write to **President@CCUniversity.edu**.

....